Warman's

World Coins

FIELD GUIDE

Arlyn G. Sieber

Values and Identification

©2010 Krause Publications, Inc.,
a subsidiary of F+W Media, Inc.

Published by

krause publications
A subsidiary of F+W Media, Inc.

700 East State Street • Iola, WI 54990-0001
715-445-2214 • 888-457-2873
www.krausebooks.com

Our toll-free number to place an order or obtain
a free catalog is (800) 258-0929.

Library of Congress Control Number: 2009937516

ISBN-13: 978-1-4402-0555-2

ISBN-10: 1-4402-0555-8

Designed by Katrina Newby
Edited by Justin Moen

Printed in China

CONTENTS

ABBREVIATIONS

AG: About Good
AL: Aluminum
ALB: Aluminum-Bronze
AU: About Uncirculated
B: Brass
BU: Brilliant Uncirculated
BV: Bullion Value
C: Copper
CN: Copper-Nickel
CNZ: Nickel-Silver
(a copper-nickel-zinc alloy)
EF: Extra Fine
F: Fine
G: Good or Gold
l.: Left
MS: Mint State

N: Nickel
NB: Nickel-Brass
ND: Not Dated
Obv.: Obverse (heads)
PF: Proof
Rev.: Reverse (tails)
r.: Right
S: Silver
St.: Steel
Unc.: Uncirculated
VF: Very Fine
VG: Very Good
WM: White Metal (a tin alloy)
XF: Extra Fine
Z: Zinc

INTRODUCTION

This book provides an overview of world coins dated 1901-2000 in an easily portable format. The values listed are approximate retail prices collectors can expect to pay for coins in commonly collected grades. Accompanying illustrations may not be actual size.

Elizabeth II 1967 25 Cents

Austria 1946 Schilling

COIN COLLECTING ONLINE

More and more numismatic sales are transacted over the Internet, but it remains a secondary market. Most dealers have created Web sites with varying results. Also, there are a couple of services that consolidate a number of dealers' offerings into a series of pages in a common location for ease of searching.

Many of the criteria you would apply to shop, mail order and show dealers can be applied to Internet dealers. Many of the more serious dealers on the Web also advertise in traditional media, permitting you to check with those periodicals. Also, the importance of membership in a professional organization still applies. Ask how long the dealer has been in business, not just collecting coins as a hobbyist. A collector who is willing to do some research and ask the right questions should find several dealers in whom they can place their confidence.

The thousands of numismatic Web sites are great resources. Not only do the nation's most important numismatic organizations have Web sites, but many local coin clubs do as well. Some can be found through the American Numismatic Association's Web site (www.money.org). Discussion groups can also provide interesting conversations normally only possible at larger coin shows.

Many of the world's largest mints have sites, including the following:

United States Mint (www.usmint.gov)
Royal Canadian Mint (www.rcmint.ca)
British Royal Mint (www.royalmint.com)

The following clubs and associations also have Web sites:
American Numismatic Association
818 North Cascade Ave.
Colorado Springs, CO 80903
www.money.org

American Numismatic Society
75 Varick St., 11th Floor
New York, NY 10013
www.numismatics.org

Canadian Numismatic Association
5694 Highway #7 East, Suite 432
Markham, ON
Canada L3P 1B4
www.canadian-numismatic.org

Sociedad Numismática de México A.C.
Eugenia 13 - 301
C.P. 03810
México, D.F., Mexico
sonumex@snm.org.mx

Florida United Numismatists
P.O. Box 5506
Titusville, FL 32783
www.funtopics.com

Central States Numismatic Society
P.O. Box 841
Logansport, IN 46947
www.centralstates.info

Great Eastern Numismatic Association
1805 Weatherstone Drive
Paoli, PA 19301

New England Numismatic Association
P.O. Box 920586
Needham, MA 02492-0007
www.nenacoin.org

Pacific Northwest Numismatic Association
P.O. Box 2210
North Bend, WA 98045
www.pnna.org

There are also many state and local organizations, too numerous to list here. Many are ANA members, so check the ANA Web site for contact information, or ask at a local library or coin shop.

HANDLING AND TREATMENT OF COINS

The first lesson of coin collecting is never touch a coin on its surface. If one needs to pick up a coin with bare hands, touch only its edge. In the case of proof coins, even greater precaution must be taken. The highly reflective surfaces are so sensitive that one should avoid even breathing directly on a coin. Doing so creates small black dots that collectors call "carbon spots." Also, do not expose coins to dust, sunlight or temperature extremes.

There are rare exceptions when it is beneficial, but generally, never clean a coin. More harm than good will likely result.

If it's necessary to handle a coin, hold it by its edge only.

COIN STORAGE

Coins can be stored in many ways. One of the most convenient is in two-inch square plastic "flips." These are transparent holders with two pockets—one for the coin and one for a cardboard ticket on which information can be recorded. It folds over on itself into a size two inches by two inches. Originally, they were made only of a material containing polyvinylchloride. This material was particularly flexible and easy to work with, but eventually it would break down, depositing a green slime on the coins it contained.

Today flips containing both the PVC formula and a new, more inert Mylar formula are available. The Mylar type is prone to cracking but so far has not been found to damage coins. The PVC type is still popular because it is more flexible, but it is now usually used by dealers and auction houses for temporary storage only. For long-term storage, the coins should be moved into inert holders.

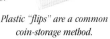

Plastic "flips" are a common coin-storage method.

Another common coin holder is the "2-by-2." It consists of a pair of cardboard squares with an adhering film of relatively inert plastic on one side. The coin is sandwiched between the two layers of plastic, and the two halves are stapled together. Be careful when removing a coin from a 2-by-2 so you don't scratch it on the exposed ends of the staples that poke out when the holder is pulled apart.

Flips and 2-by-2s fit nicely in specially made boxes. They also fit into plastic pages designed to hold 20 of either holder. The pages are transparent and will fit into most loose-leaf binders. Do not place coins loose in the actual pages because they often contain PVC. Moreover, the thumb-cuts made to help remove the coins are large enough for some coins to fall through.

Many specialized coin folders and albums are designed not only to store and exhibit a collection but also to guide collectors. Each spot for a coin in the series is labeled.

Store coins in a cool, dry, and secure environment. A bank safe-deposit box provides the most security. If you live in a humid climate, include a packet of silica gel in the box or other container holding your coins. The gel is a desiccant and will absorb the moisture from the air. The packets can sometimes be obtained at photo shops if your local coin dealer does not stock them.

The 2-by-2 holder is another popular coin-storage method.

DETECTING COUNTERFEITS

There are different types of counterfeit coins created for different purposes, but the type of most concern to collectors is "numismatic counterfeits." These are high-quality fakes created with great care to fool numismatic experts. Many counterfeits are made by casting, even though the original coin may have been struck. Look for seams along the edge. They may not be centered and obvious but can be hidden to one side or the other. Also, examine the surface under magnification for a multitude of faint pimples or unnatural porosity. Imprecise shaping in the letters on a coin can also signal a counterfeit. On modern coins, an inaccurate weight or incorrect alloy (revealed by specific-gravity testing) can be a giveaway. Many counterfeiters try to hide their coins' imperfections with heavy cleaning.

A good magnifying glass is an essential tool for coin collectors.

CONDITION AND GRADING

A coin's value is determined in part by its "grade," or how well preserved it is. The most basic part of grading is determining how much a coin is worn. Numismatists have agreed on a series of terms to describe the amount of wear. Unlike U.S. and Canadian coins, there are few grading guides for world coins. Following are some general standards that should prove useful for most coins. In grading world coins, there are two main factors to consider: (1) loss of design details, such as hair, feathers, designs on coats of arms, or beads on the arches of a crown, and (2) how well the coin was struck.

Uncirculated (Unc.) coins have no wear, as though they just came from the mint. Even a magnifying glass should reveal no evidence of wear.

Brilliant Uncirculated (BU) means a mint-state coin that still has its original bright mint luster.

About Uncirculated (AU) describes coins with such slight signs of wear that a mild magnifying glass may be needed to see them. A trace of luster should be visible.

Extremely Fine (EF, XF) is the highest-grade coin that exhibits wear heavy enough to be seen easily by the unaided eye. Ninety to 95 percent of the minute details will still be extremely sharp and clear. Many will exhibit luster, but it is not required.

Very Fine (VF) coins show obvious signs of wear, but most design detail will still be clear. It is an overall pleasant coin.

Fine (F) is the lowest grade most people would consider collectible. About half the design details remain. All lettering should be legible but may be somewhat weak.

Very Good (VG) coins exhibit heavy wear. All design outlines are clear, as is generally the rim. Perhaps a quarter of the internal details will also show, but most will be worn off.

Good (G) coins are generally considered uncollectible except for novelty purposes. There will be little or no internal detail to the design. Some of the rim may also be worn out.

About Good (AG) and **Fair (Fr)** are grades in which only scarce coins are collected. Many collectors would rather do without a coin in these grades than add it to their collections. The rim will be worn down, and some outline to the design may be gone.

Proof describes a special way of making coins for presentation. A proof coin is usually double struck with highly polished dies on polished blanks, which produces a mirror-like finish.

Proof 1996 Barbados five-dollar coin.

COIN MARKET UPDATE

Rising prices for gold and silver bullion are the dominant factors affecting the coin market. The result is an overall increase in values for gold and silver coins.

In September 2009, gold broke $1,000 a troy ounce. At the same time, silver was trading for more than $17 a troy ounce.

Bullion prices form the base value for any coin composed of gold or silver. At the least, a coin composed of either metal is worth its intrinsic value—the amount of pure gold or silver contained in the coin (in troy ounces) times the current trading price for gold or silver bullion. Thus, rising gold and silver bullion prices generally mean rising gold and silver coin prices.

Values for some gold and silver coins are based solely on their bullion value. These include Canada's Maple Leaf series and South Africa's Krugerrand series, and older issues of originally general-circulation coins with ample supplies available in today's collector market. Other gold and silver coins may trade for a small premium above their bullion value, such as five percent.

Many daily newspapers report precious-metals prices in the financial sections of their print editions and Web sites. Among them is USA Today. Go to www.usatoday.com, click on Money, then Markets, and then Commodities.

CANADIAN COINS

Like Colonial American and early Mexican coinage, Canadian money before the 1870s was a hodgepodge of various coins and tokens struck by a number of authorities, firms, countries, and individuals. Throughout the 1700s and early 1800s, the British policies of mercantilism prevented the royal government from shipping reasonable quantities of sterling to British North America. By the time the idea was seriously considered, there was already chaos.

When official coinage was finally struck by the various pre-confederation colonial provinces, they had already recognized slightly different standards, sometimes as much as 20-percent difference in value. The first coins struck in the name of Canada were produced by the province of Canada. This was the collective name for Upper Canada (Ontario) and Lower Canada (Quebec). Bronze cents and silver 5-cent, 10-cent, and 20-cent pieces were struck in 1858-59. In the intervening years before these two provinces combined with New Brunswick and Nova Scotia to form the independent Canadian confederation in 1867, all of them had struck their own coins. Despite this complexity of coinage, a shortage of small change still persisted. Neither bank tokens nor poorly made "blacksmith" counterfeits could be suppressed.

During the American Civil War, when U.S. silver coins were being discounted in terms of gold, some firms bought them up in quantity and imported them. Unfortunately, it soon became the tool of scams, whereby they were paid out at par but taken for deposit only at a discount. Finally, in 1869-70, a three-step program was devised to cure this dilemma.

The U.S. silver was bought up, and $4 million worth was sent back south. An order was placed with the Royal Mint for millions of new sterling-silver Canadian 5-cent, 10-cent, 25-cent, and 50-cent pieces. Last, a temporary issue of fractional paper money redeemable in gold was released to make due until the new coins arrived. (This small paper money proved so popular that it continued to be issued until the 1930s.)

The new Canadian silver coins, nominally valued at one U.S. dollar worth of gold per Canadian dollar, were struck in quantity except during the depression of the late 1870s. They were supplemented by a large initial issue of cents in 1876. These were slightly heavier than the province's old cents and continued from 1881 onward. The standards for cents and silver remained unchanged until World War I.

During the 1800s, Canadian coins were struck at the Royal Mint in London and sometimes by contract at the Heaton Mint in Birmingham, England. In 1908, after years of agitation, a branch of the Royal Mint was opened in Ottawa. With it came the ability to mint the gold being mined in Canada into internationally recognized British-design sovereigns. Soon after that, a domestic gold coinage was initiated.

The basic designs for most Canadian coins remained fairly stable from the beginning until 1937, but many smaller changes occurred as needed. Of course, with the passing of each monarch, a new royal portrait was designed—one for Edward VII in 1902, another for George V in 1911. The gold sovereigns used bareheaded busts instead of crowned ones to match their British counterparts. There was a bit of a ruckus in 1911 when the new obverse of George V lacked the Latin phrase Dei Gratia ("by the grace of God"). The mint responded to the public outcry and added the phrase the following year.

World War I and its aftermath resulted in more modifications. The large cent was replaced in 1920 by a small cent, and in 1922, the silver 5-cent was replaced by a nickel 5-cent. Both were similar in size to their American counterparts. Also, as a result of a wartime increase in silver prices, the alloy of coins in that metal was reduced from 92-1/2 percent (sterling) to 80 percent beginning with 1920.

The entire visual style of Canadian coins changed in 1935, when a new, artistic commemorative silver dollar for the jubilee of George V was released. It depicted the now famous design of a fur trapper and an Indian paddling a canoe. When the obverses were changed to portray the new King George VI in 1937, the opportunity was taken to revise all the reverses of the smaller denominations with creative and distinctly Canadian designs. The cent was given a more naturalistic sprig of maple leaves, the 5-cent a beaver on its dam, the 10-cent a schooner, and the 25-cent the bust of a caribou. The 50-cent coins displayed a more conservative coat of arms. Because of the time taken to design the new coinage, some 1936-dated coins were struck in 1937. Their design included a minute dot to distinguish them. These are quite rare. The reverses introduced in 1937 continue in use today with some alteration.

World War II brought more changes to Canadian coins. Shortages of nickel caused the 5-cent piece to be struck in a brass alloy called tombac and later in chromium-plated steel. It was finally restored to its nickel composition in 1955. A special reverse design—a torch superimposed on a V for victory—was used to boost wartime morale. Because of the time taken to modify the royal titles to reflect the independence of India, some 1947 coins were struck in 1948 with a tiny maple leaf after the date. Although not rare, these are quite popular.

No monarch has had as many different portraits on Canadian coins as Elizabeth II. The first portrait, designed by Mary Gillick, had some minor difficulties in striking and, as a result, was subtly modified after being placed in production. In 1965 a new bust wearing a tiara was introduced, years before Britain itself began using it. When a mature head of the queen was desired, the Canadian choice for the first time differed from that of Britain. A design with an open crown, by Canadian artist Dora de Pédery-Hunt was used beginning in 1990. It was replaced in mid-2003 by a bareheaded, grandmotherly portrait designed by Susanna Blunt.

The centennial of Canadian independence was cause for issue of some of the country's most beautiful and dignified wildlife coins. Animals emblematic of Canada shown against stark open backgrounds were portrayed on the reverses of the 1967 issues, along with a gold $20 piece with the national arms. Unfortunately, the rising price of silver forced these animal coins out of circulation. In mid-year, the 10-cent and 25-cent pieces were reduced to 50-percent silver, and beginning in 1968, pure nickel replaced all circulating silver.

Throughout the 1970s to the 1990s, various modifications were made to reduce the expense of producing coins, which were no longer tied to their intrinsic value. The cent went through several modifications in weight and shape before it was switched to copper-plated zinc in 1997. It was later supplemented by issues in copper-plated steel. In 1982, the 5-cent piece was changed from nickel to cupronickel, then to nickel-plated steel in 2000, along with the 10-cent, 25-cent, and 50-cent pieces. Radical new $1 and $2 coins were introduced to save the expense of producing less durable paper money. A small, golden, bronze-plated nickel dollar depicting a swimming loon was introduced in 1987. In 1996 a $2 coin depicting a polar bear and composed of a nickel ring surrounding an aluminum bronze center followed. Today these two coins are popularly known as the "loonie" and "twonie" respectively.

Since the 1970s Canada has had an aggressive collector coin program, with several different designs in various precious metal offered in quality strikes each year. Some of these are quite scarce and are made in limited quantities. Others, however, particularly those of the 1970s, are so common they are frequently melted for scrap. Some of the more unusual pieces are the silver aviation series, which boasts a small portrait inlay of gold. This decade also saw the old cellophane-packaged proof-like sets supplemented with the more market-oriented cased proof sets.

Circulating commemoratives were struck for the 125th anniversary of the Canadian confederation in 1992. Most coins just bore the "1867-1992" legend, but a popular series of 25-cent coins bore reverses emblematic of each province and territory. A dollar depicting children before Parliament was issued as well.

Canada is one of the world's richest nations in terms of precious metals and for years has produced some of the world's most popular bullion coins. Silver one-ounce, gold 1/20-ounce to one-ounce, and platinum 1/20-ounce to one-ounce pieces are struck bearing an intricate and difficult to counterfeit maple leaf reverse.

CANADIAN MINTMARKS

C	Ottawa, Ontario
H	Heaton, Birmingham, England
none (1858-1907)	Royal Mint, London
none (1908-)	Ottawa, Ontario
none (1968)	Philadelphia (U.S.)
none (1973-)	Hull, Quebec
none (1975-)	Winnipeg, Manitoba
P (1999-)	Plated on steel blank
W (1998-)	Winnipeg, Manitoba

GRADING CANADIAN COINS

Certain convenient key reference points facilitate the grading of Canadian coins. On Queen Victoria's portraits, it is the hair over the ear or braid below the ear. For issues depicting Edward VII and George V, it is the band of the crown.

Even though the reverse of a pre-1937 Canadian coin is usually in better grade than the obverse, the value of a coin in the marketplace is primarily determined by the grade of its obverse. Also, pure-nickel George V 5-cent pieces are difficult to grade. Because of nickel's hardness, the dies did not always leave a sharp impression. Thus, an understanding of the metal's texture and surface is useful in grading this series.

Uncirculated coins with particularly unpleasant bag marks, color, or toning may trade at a heavy discount.

MS-65 or Gem—This is the highest grade one is likely to encounter. It has no wear and no significant bag marks, particularly in open areas such as the field or cheek. Copper must have luster.

MS-63 or Choice Uncirculated—This is a pleasant coin with no wear but enough bag marks to be noticed. Still, the bag marks are few enough that the coin is not considered marred, particularly in open areas such as the field or cheek.

MS-60 or Uncirculated—Although there is no wear on an MS-60 coin, it is not necessarily attractive. It will bear scuffs and bag marks acquired from handling at the mint before release. Copper will usually be toned, and some coins of either metal may be discolored.

AU or Almost Uncirculated—This describes a coin with such slight signs of wear that a mild magnifying glass may be needed to see them. One should be careful not to confuse an attractive AU coin for uncirculated. Look for the texture of the metal.

XF or Extremely Fine—This is the highest grade of coin that exhibits wear significant enough to be seen easily by the unaided eye. It still exhibits clear minute detail. In the case of Victorian coins, the hair over the ear and jewels of the diadem, or segments of braid, are sharp. In the case of Edward VII and George V coins, the jewels in the band of the crown are sharp. George VI coins will have only the slightest wear in the hair over the ear.

VF or Very Fine—These coins show obvious signs of wear. Nevertheless, most of the design detail is still clear. In the case of Victorian coins, the hair over the ear, or segments of braid, are visible but not sharp. The same is true of the jewels in the diadem. In the case of Edward VII and George V, the jewels in the band of the crown are visible but not sharp. George VI coins will have about 80 percent of hair detail visible.

F or Fine—This is the lowest grade most people consider collectible. About half the design detail will show for most types. In the case of Victorian coins, the strands of the hair over the ear, or segments of braid, begin to run into each other. Some of the details in the diadem will be obscured. In the case of Edward VII and George V coins, the jewels in the band of the crown will be unclear, but the band will be distinct from the head. George VI coins will have only about half the hair detail visible.

VG or Very Good—These coins exhibit heavy wear. All outlines are clear, as is generally the rim. Some internal detail will also show, but most will be worn off. On Victorian coins, the details in the strands of the hair over the ear or segments of braid will be obscured. Most details in the diadem will be obscured. In the case of Edward VII and George V coins, the band of the crown will be worn through at its center. George VI coins will have only about one-third of the hair detail visible.

G or Good—These coins are generally considered uncollectible except for novelty purposes. There will usually be little or no internal detail to the design. Some of the rim may also be barely visible on silver. With Victorian coins, the hair over the ear or the braid will be mostly obscured, as will the majority of the diadem. On Edward VII and George V coins, the band of the crown will be worn through along most of its width. George VI coins will have no hair detail.

CENTS

One-inch-wide large cents were among the first coins struck by the province of Canada in 1858-59 before the formation of the confederation. These coins, with a young head of Queen Victoria, were struck in large quantities and were still in bank coffers until 1875. The following year, another large order for cents was placed, this time with a heavier weight and a mature head of the queen. This order lasted for five years. Since 1881, Canadian cents have been struck almost continuously.

With the passing of Queen Victoria, a new portrait was designed for Edward VII in 1902 and another for George V in 1911. When the obverse was changed to portray the new King George VI in 1937, the reverse of the cent was revised also. It was given a more naturalistic sprig of maple leaves, designed by G.E. Kruger-Gray. Because of the time taken to design the new cents, some 1936-dated coins were struck in 1937 bearing a minute dot to distinguish them. These are quite rare. The reverse introduced in 1937, with some alteration, continues today.

Because of the time taken to modify the royal titles to reflect the independence of India, some 1947 cents were struck in 1948 with a tiny maple leaf after the date. Although not rare, these are quite popular.

No monarch has had as many different portraits on Canadian coins as Elizabeth II. The first portrait, designed by Mary Gillick, had some minor difficulties in striking and, as a result, was subtly modified after production began. In 1965 a new bust wearing a tiara was introduced, years before Britain itself began using it. When a mature head of the queen was desired, the Canadian choice differed from that of Britain. A design with an open crown, by Canadian artist Dora de Pédery-Hunt, was used beginning in 1990. It was replaced in mid-2003 by a bareheaded, grandmotherly portrait designed by Susanna Blunt.

As part of a set of wildlife coins struck for the centennial of Canadian independence, the 1967 cent depicted a rock dove. For its 125th anniversary, the dual date "1867-1992" was used.

In an economy measure, the cent's weight was reduced in 1979, 1980 and 1982. Its copper alloy was switched to copperplated zinc in 1997. In most years since 1999, these cents were supplemented by examples struck in copper-plated steel. The latter are marked with a "P" on the obverse. From 1982 to 1996, Canadian cents were 12-sided.

Known Counterfeits: The 1936 dot variety is a prime target.

VICTORIA	VG	VF
1901	2.25	4.50

Edward VII 1905 Large Cent

EDWARD VII	VG	VF
1902	1.75	3.50
1903	1.75	3.00
1904	2.00	5.00
1905	3.50	7.50
1906	1.75	3.00
1907	2.00	4.50
1907H	12.00	30.00
1908	3.00	5.00
1909	1.75	3.00
1910	1.75	3.00
GEORGE V—LARGE SIZE	F	XF
1911	1.30	3.50
1912	1.50	3.50
1913	1.50	4.00
1914	1.50	4.00
1915	2.25	4.00
1916	.65	3.00
1917	.65	2.25
1918	.65	2.25
1919	.65	2.25
1920	.75	2.25

George V 1911 Large Cent

George V 1920 Small Cent

GEORGE V—SMALL SIZE	F	XF
1920	.50	2.00
1921	.75	5.00
1922	16.00	35.00
1923	35.00	50.00
1924	6.50	15.00
1925	21.00	40.00
1926	4.50	11.00
1927	2.00	6.00
1928	.30	1.50
1929	.30	1.50
1930	2.50	8.50
1931	1.00	5.50
1932	.20	1.50
1933	.30	1.50
1934	.30	1.50
1935	.30	1.50
1936	.30	1.50
1936, dot below date	rare	

George VI 1938 Cent

GEORGE VI	XF	MS-63
1937	2.00	9.00
1938	.75	13.00
1939	.70	5.00
1940	.50	5.50
1941	.50	60.00
1942	.50	60.00
1943	.45	25.00
1944	.60	100.00
1945	.35	22.00
1946	.35	7.50
1947	.35	7.50
1947, maple leaf	.35	5.00
1948	.70	35.00
1949	.35	9.00
1950	.25	9.00
1951	.20	13.00
1952	.20	7.00

ELIZABETH II	MS-63
1953, without shoulder strap	1.50
1953, with strap	55.00
1954, without strap, proof-like	500.00
1954, with strap	6.00
1955, without strap	1,800.00
1955, with strap	1.50
1956	.90
1957	.60
1958	.60
1959	.30
1960	.30
1961	.30
1962	.30
1963	.30
1964	.30
1965	.20
1966	.20
1967, centennial	.20
1968	.15
1969	.15
1970	.15
1971	.15
1972	.15

Elizabeth II 1994 Cent

ELIZABETH II	MS-63
1973	.15
1974	.15
1975	.15
1976	.15
1977	.15
1978	.15
1979	.15
1980	.15
1981	.15
1982	.15
1983	.15
1984	.15
1985	.15
1986	.15
1987	.15
1988	.15
1989	.15
1990	.15
1991	.15
1992, "1867-1992"	.15
1993	.15

ELIZABETH II	MS-63
1994	.15
1995	.15
1996	.15
Copper-plated zinc and copper-plated steel.	
1997	.15
1998	.15
1998, bronze in sets only	.75
1998W	1.75
1999	.15
1999P	6.00
2000	.15
2000, proof-like	1.75
2000, "1908-1998" large cent, PF	16.00

Elizabeth II 1998 Cent

FIVE CENTS

Tiny sterling-silver 5-cent pieces were among the first coins struck by the province of Canada in 1858 before the formation of the confederation. These coins bore a young head of Queen Victoria. Twelve years later, the new confederation started issuing silver 5-cent coins, making no significant changes from the earlier provincial piece.

With the passing of Queen Victoria, a new portrait was designed for Edward VII in 1902, followed the next year by a change on the reverse from St. Edward's crown to the imperial crown. There was a bit of a ruckus in 1911 when the new obverse with George V's portrait lacked the Latin phrase Dei Gratia ("by the grace of God"). The mint responded to the public outcry, and beginning in 1912, these titles were added.

As a result of a World War I increase in silver prices, the alloy was reduced from 92.5 percent pure (sterling) to 80 percent in 1920. Public complaint persisted about this coin's small size. Not only were they prone to loss and fumbling, their thinness resulted in dents, edge dings, and bends, which collectors object to today. It was replaced in 1922 by a larger coin much like America's but composed of pure nickel.

When the obverse was changed to portray the new King George VI in 1937, the reverse was revised also. A beaver on its dam was portrayed, designed by G.E. Kruger-Gray. This new reverse, with some alteration, is still used today.

World War II also brought changes to Canadian coins. Shortages of nickel caused the 5-cent piece to be struck in a brass alloy called tombac in 1942-44 and in chromium-plated steel in 1944-45 and 1951-54. A special reverse design—a torch superimposed on a V for victory—was used to boost wartime morale.

Because of the time taken to modify the royal titles to reflect the independence of India, some 1947 coins were struck in 1948 with a tiny dot or maple leaf after the date. The dot is scarce, the leaf common, but both are quite popular.

No monarch has had as many different portraits on Canadian coins as Elizabeth II. The first portrait, designed by Mary Gillick, had some minor difficulties in striking and, as a result, was subtly modified after production began. In 1965, a new bust wearing a tiara was introduced, years before Britain itself began using it. When a mature head of the queen was desired, the Canadian choice differed from that of Britain. A design with an open crown, by Canadian artist Dora de Pédery-Hunt, was used beginning in 1990. It was replaced in mid-2003 by a bareheaded, grandmotherly portrait designed by Susanna Blunt.

As part of a set of wildlife coins struck for the centennial of Canadian independence, the 1967 5-cent piece depicted a rabbit running. For its 125th anniversary, the dual date "1867-1992" was displayed. Recently, a series of 5-cent pieces with commemorative reverses has been struck in silver.

In an economy measure, the alloy of the 5-cent coin was changed to 75-percent copper, 25-percent nickel in 1982. It was switched to nickel-plated steel gradually from 1999 to 2001.

VICTORIA	VG	VF
1901	4.50	12.00

Victoria 1901 5 Cents

EDWARD VII	VG	VF
1902	2.25	4.00
1902H, broad H	2.25	5.50
1902H, narrow H	7.50	24.00
1903	4.00	17.00
1903H	1.75	7.00
1904	2.75	7.00
1905	1.75	9.00
1906	2.25	6.00
1907	2.25	4.00
1908	6.00	23.00
1909	3.00	10.00
1910	2.25	5.00

Edward VII 1910 5 Cents

George V Silver 1911 5 Cents

GEORGE V—SILVER	VG	VF
1911	2.00	9.00
1912	2.00	9.00
1913	2.00	7.50
1914	2.00	9.00
1915	11.00	50.00
1916	2.75	22.00
1917	1.75	7.00
1918	1.75	6.50
1919	1.75	6.50
1920	1.75	6.50
1921	2,700.00	6,750.00
GEORGE V—NICKEL	VG	VF
1922	.35	7.00
1923	.40	16.00
1924	.50	10.00
1925	55.00	200.00
1926, near 6	3.00	60.00
1926, far 6	100.00	600.00
1927	.35	15.00
1928	.35	15.00
1929	.35	15.00
1930	.35	15.00
1931	.35	18.00

George V Nickel 1927 5 Cents

GEORGE V—NICKEL	VG	VF
1932	.35	16.00
1933	.40	18.00
1934	.35	16.00
1935	.35	11.00
1936	.35	9.00
GEORGE VI	**XF**	**Unc.**
1937	2.50	9.00
1938	7.00	75.00
1939	3.00	45.00
1940	2.25	18.00
1941	2.25	23.00
1942, nickel	1.75	18.00
1942, brass	1.75	3.00
1943, brass	.80	3.00
1944, brass	unique	
1944, steel	.90	2.00
1945, steel	.80	2.00
1946	2.00	14.00
1947	1.25	10.00
1947, dot	60.00	175.00
1947, maple leaf	1.25	10.00
1948	3.00	18.00
1949	.75	6.00

George VI 1947 5 Cents

GEORGE VI	XF	Unc.
1950	.75	6.00
1951, steel	.80	3.50
1951, nickel	.45	1.75
1952, steel	.80	3.00
ELIZABETH II		BU
1953, steel, without strap		7.00
1953, steel, with strap		7.00
1954, steel		8.00
1955		4.50
1956		5.00
1957		3.00
1958		3.00
1959		1.50
1960		1.50
1961		.80
1962		.80
1963		.75
1964		.75
1965		.30
1966		.30
1967, centennial		.40
1968		.30
1969		.30

ELIZABETH II	BU
1970	.75
1971	.30
1972	.30
1973	.30
1974	.30
1975	.30
1976	.30
1977	.30
1978	.30
1979	.30
1980	.30
1981	.30
Cupronickel	
1982	.30
1983	.30
1984	.30
1985	.30
1986	.30
1987	.30
1988	.30
1989	.30
1990	.30
1991	.55

Elizabeth II 2000 5 Cents

ELIZABETH II	BU
1992, "1867-1992"	.30
1993	.30
1994	.30
1995	.30
1996	2.25
1996, silver, PF	5.00
1997	.30
1997, silver, PF	5.00
1998	.30
1998, silver, PF	5.00
1998W	1.50
1998, "1908-1998," silver	12.00
1999	.30
1999, silver, PF	5.00
1999P	15.00
2000	.30
2000, silver, PF	5.00
2000P	3.50
2000W	1.50
2000, Voltigeurs, silver, PF	9.00

TEN CENTS

Sterling-silver 10-cent pieces were among the first coins struck by the province of Canada in 1858 before the formation of the confederation. These coins bore a young head of Queen Victoria. Twelve years later the new confederation started issuing silver 10-cent coins, making no significant changes from the earlier provincial piece.

With the passing of Queen Victoria, a new portrait was designed for Edward VII in 1902. There was a bit of a ruckus in 1911 when the new obverse with George V's portrait lacked the Latin phrase Dei Gratia ("by the grace of God"). The mint responded to the public outcry, and beginning in 1912, these titles were added.

As a result of a World War I increase in silver prices, the alloy was reduced from 92.5 percent pure (sterling) to 80 percent beginning in 1920.

When the obverse was changed to portray the new King George VI in 1937, the reverse of the 10-cent piece was revised also. A fishing schooner under sail is depicted, designed by Emanuel Hahn. Because of the time required to design the new reverse, some 1936-dated coins were struck in 1937 bearing a minute dot to distinguish them. These are quite rare. This new reverse is, with some alteration, still used today.

Because of the time required to modify the royal titles on the dies to reflect the independence of India, some 1947 coins were struck in 1948 with a maple leaf after the date. These are common but are quite popular.

No monarch has had as many different portraits on Canadian coins as Elizabeth II. The first portrait, designed by Mary Gillick, had some minor difficulties in striking and, as a result, was subtly modified after being placed in production. In 1965 a new bust wearing a tiara was introduced, years before Britain itself began using it. When a mature head of the queen was desired, the Canadian choice differed from that of Britain. A design with an open crown, by Canadian artist Dora de Pédery-Hunt, was used beginning in 1990. It was replaced in mid-2003 by a bareheaded, grandmotherly portrait designed by Susanna Blunt.

As part of a set of wildlife coins struck for the centennial of Canadian independence, the 1967 10-cent piece depicted a mackerel. Unfortunately, the rising price of silver forced the centennial coins out of circulation. In mid-year the 10-cent piece was reduced to 50-percent silver and, beginning in 1968, to pure nickel. It was switched to nickel-plated steel in 2001, with proofs struck in sterling.

For the confederation's 125th anniversary, the dual date "1867-1992" was displayed on the regular type. The 1997 issue, commemorating the voyages of John Cabot, began a series of commemorative 10-cent pieces.

Modern counting machines occasionally leave a circular scratch on these coins, and these damaged coins are virtually worthless unless they are scarcer dates.

Known Counterfeits: The 1936 dot should be examined by an expert. 1930 circulation counterfeits are known.

VICTORIA	VG	VF
1901	8.50	40.00

Edward VII 1902H 10 Cents

EDWARD VII	VG	VF
1902	8.00	30.00
1902H	4.00	18.00
1903	14.00	75.00
1903H	7.00	30.00
1904	11.00	45.00
1905	6.50	55.00
1906	6.50	30.00
1907	4.25	23.00
1908	8.00	55.00
1909, Victorian leaves	6.00	40.00
1909, broad leaves	10.00	55.00
1910	4.00	18.00
GEORGE V	VG	XF
1911	4.50	40.00
1912	1.75	30.00
1913, large leaves	95.00	900.00
1913, small leaves	1.50	23.00
1914	1.50	25.00
1915	6.00	100.00
1916	1.25	17.00
1917	1.25	10.00
1918	1.25	9.00
1919	1.25	9.00

GEORGE V	VG	XF
1920	1.00	12.00
1921	1.25	20.00
1928	1.00	12.00
1929	1.00	12.00
1930	1.00	14.00
1931	1.00	12.00
1932	1.50	23.00
1933	2.00	35.00
1934	3.00	60.00
1935	3.50	60.00
1936	1.00	9.00
1936, dot	four known	

George V 1931 10 Cents

GEORGE VI	XF	Unc.
1937	3.75	12.00
1938	6.50	40.00
1939	5.00	45.00
1940	3.00	15.00
1941	6.00	35.00
1942	4.00	30.00
1943	4.00	18.00
1944	4.50	25.00
1945	4.00	18.00
1946	4.50	30.00
1947	6.00	30.00
1947, maple leaf	3.00	10.00
1948	13.00	45.00
1949	2.00	9.00
1950	1.50	8.00
1951	1.50	6.00
1952	1.50	5.00

George VI 1948 10 Cents

ELIZABETH II	XF	BU
1953, without straps	1.25	6.00
1953, with straps	1.25	8.00
1954	2.25	17.00
1955	1.00	7.00
1956	1.00	6.00
1956, dot below date	4.50	22.00
1957	—	3.00
1958	—	3.00
1959	—	3.00
1960	—	2.25
1961	—	2.25
1962	—	1.50
1963	—	1.50
1964	—	1.50
1965	—	1.50
1966	—	1.50
1967, centennial	—	1.50
1968	—	1.25
Nickel		
1968		.35
1969		.35
1970		.90
1971		.35

ELIZABETH II	BU
1972	.35
1973	.35
1974	.35
1975	.35
1976	.35
1977	.35
1978	.35
1979	.35
1980	.35
1981	.35
1982	.35
1983	.35
1984	.35
1985	.35
1986	.35
1987	.35
1988	.35
1989	.35
1990	.35
1991	.45
1992, "1867-1992"	.35
1993	.35
1994	.35

ELIZABETH II	BU
1995	.35
1996	.35
1996, silver, PF	5.50
1997	.35
1997, silver, PF	5.50
1997, John Cabot, silver, PF	17.50
1998	.35
1998, silver, PF	4.00
1998O, silver, PF	4.00
1998W	1.50
1998, "1908-1998," silver, PF	10.00
1999	.35
1999, silver, PF	5.00
1999P	15.00
2000	.35
2000, silver, PF	5.00
2000P	1,000.00
2000W	1.50
2000, first Canadian credit union, silver, PF	8.00

TWENTY-FIVE CENTS

Sterling-silver 25-cent pieces were first struck in 1870 after it was decided to abandon the old 20-cent denomination. The new coin was more similar to the U.S. quarters that were imported into Canada during the U.S. Civil War. The Canadian 25-cent coins bore an older head of Queen Victoria. They saw hard service and were not replaced as they wore out. Hence, they can be difficult to find in middle to upper grades.

With the passing of Queen Victoria, a new portrait was designed for Edward VII in 1902. There was a bit of a ruckus in 1911 when the new obverse with George V's portrait lacked the Latin phrase Dei Gratia ("by the grace of God"). The mint responded to the public outcry, and beginning in 1912, these titles were added.

Because of a World War I increase in silver prices, the alloy was reduced from 92.5 percent pure (sterling) to 80 percent beginning with 1920.

When the obverse was changed to portray the new King George VI in 1937, the opportunity was taken to revise the reverse of the 25-cent piece. A caribou's bust is depicted, designed by Emanuel Hahn. Because of the time taken to design the new reverse, some 1936-dated coins were struck in 1937 bearing a minute dot to distinguish them. These are quite rare. This reverse is, with some alteration, still used today.

Because of the time required to modify the royal titles on the dies to reflect the independence of India, some 1947 coins were struck in 1948 with a tiny dot or maple leaf after the date. The dot variety is scarce; the leaf variety is not. But both are quite popular.

No monarch has had as many different portraits on Canadian coins as Elizabeth II. The first portrait, designed by Mary Gillick, had some minor difficulties in striking and, as a result, was subtly modified after production began. In 1965 a new bust wearing a tiara was introduced, years before Britain itself began using it. When a mature head of the queen was desired, the Canadian choice differed from that of Britain. A design with an open crown, by Canadian artist Dora de Pédery-Hunt, was used beginning in 1990. It was replaced in mid-2003 by a bareheaded, grandmotherly portrait designed by Susanna Blunt.

As part of a set of wildlife coins struck for the centennial of Canadian independence, the 1967 25-cent piece depicted a bobcat. Unfortunately, the rising price of silver forced the centennial coins out of circulation.

In mid-year this coin was reduced to 50-percent silver and, beginning in 1968, to pure nickel. It was switched to nickel-plated steel in 2000, with proofs struck in sterling.

A special reverse was used in 1973 to commemorate the centenary of the Royal Canadian Mounted Police. A set of circulating commemorative 25-cent pieces was struck for the

125th anniversary of the Canadian confederation in 1992. One of the coins simply bore an "1867-1992" legend, but a dozen others in the popular series bore reverses emblematic of each province and territory. A series of monthly Millennium 25-cent pieces, struck in the old nickel composition, was initiated in 1999 and 2000.

Known Counterfeits: The 1936 dot should be examined by an expert.

VICTORIA	VG	VF
1901	12.00	50.00

EDWARD VII	VG	VF
1902	10.00	65.00
1902H	6.50	45.00
1903	15.00	75.00
1904	20.00	150.00
1905	15.00	100.00
1906, small crown	2,500.00	6,000.00
1906, large crown	8.00	55.00
1907	6.50	55.00
1908	15.00	95.00
1909	12.00	70.00
1910	5.50	40.00

George V 1911 25 Cents

GEORGE V	F	XF
1911	18.00	85.00
1912	9.00	55.00
1913	8.50	50.00
1914	10.00	60.00
1915	45.00	425.00
1916	7.50	40.00
1917	6.00	30.00
1918	5.00	26.00
1919	5.00	25.00
1920	6.00	30.00
1921	24.00	225.00
1927	50.00	225.00
1928	6.00	35.00
1929	6.00	35.00
1930	6.00	40.00
1931	6.00	50.00
1932	6.00	50.00
1933	6.50	65.00
1934	9.00	70.00
1935	7.50	50.00
1936	5.00	21.00
1936, dot	65.00	300.00

George VI 1911 25 Cents

GEORGE VI	XF	Unc.
1937	6.00	16.00
1938	10.00	65.00
1939	7.00	50.00
1940	3.00	15.00
1941	3.00	16.00
1942	3.00	17.00
1943	3.00	16.00
1944	3.00	26.00
1945	3.00	16.00
1946	8.00	45.00
1947	8.00	50.00
1947, dot after date	150.00	250.00
1947, maple leaf	3.00	16.00
1948	13.00	55.00
1949	3.00	10.00
1950	2.50	8.00
1951	2.50	7.00
1952	2.50	6.00

ELIZABETH II	XF	BU
1953, without strap	2.75	10.00
1953, with strap	2.75	18.00
1954	7.00	40.00
1955	2.75	15.00
1956	2.75	6.50
1957	—	5.00
1958	—	5.00
1959	—	3.50
1960	—	3.50
1961	—	3.50
1962	—	3.50
1963	—	3.00
1964	—	3.00
1965	—	3.00
1966	—	3.00
1967, centennial	—	3.00
1968	—	3.00
Nickel		
1968		.75
1969		.75
1970		2.00
1971		.75
1972		.75

Elizabeth II 1967 25 Cents

ELIZABETH II	BU
1973, R.C.M.P.	1.00
1974	.75
1975	.75
1976	.75
1977	.75
1978	.75
1979	.75
1980	.75
1981	.75
1982	.75
1983	1.50
1984	.75
1985	.75
1986	.75
1987	1.25
1988	1.00
1989	.75
1990	.90
1991	12.00
1992, "1867-1992"	12.50
1992 Alberta	.70
1992 Alberta, silver, PF	5.50
1992 British Columbia	.70

ELIZABETH II	BU
1992 British Columbia, silver, PF	5.50
1992 Manitoba	.70
1992 Manitoba, silver, PF	5.50
1992 New Brunswick	.70
1992 New Brunswick, silver, PF	.50
1992 Newfoundland	.70
1992 Newfoundland, silver, PF	5.50
1992 Northwest Territories	.70
1992 Northwest Territories, silver, PF	5.50
1992 Nova Scotia	.70
1992 Nova Scotia, silver, PF	5.50
1992 Ontario	.70
1992 Ontario, silver, PF	5.50
1992 Prince Edward Island	.70
1992 Prince Edward Island, silver, PF	5.50
1992 Quebec	.70
1992 Quebec, silver, PF	5.50
1992 Saskatchewan	.70
1992 Saskatchewan, silver, PF	5.50
1992 Yukon	.70
1992 Yukon, silver, PF	5.50
1993	.70
1994	.70

Elizabeth II 1994 25 Cents

ELIZABETH II	BU
1995	.70
1996	.70
1996, silver, PF	6.50
1997	.70
1997, silver, PF	6.50
1998, silver, PF	5.50
1998O, silver, PF	5.50
1998W	5.00
1998, "1908-1998," silver	15.00
1999	.75
1999, silver, PF	5.50
1999P	20.00
1999 January	.65
1999 January, silver, PF	8.00
1999 February	.65
1999 February, silver, PF	8.00
1999 March	.65
1999 March, silver, PF	8.00
1999 April	.65
1999 June	.65
1999 June, silver, PF	8.00
1999 July	.65
1999 July, silver, PF	8.00

ELIZABETH II	BU
1999 August	.65
1999 August, silver, PF	8.00
1999 September	.65
1999 September, silver, PF	8.00
1999 October	.65
1999 October, silver, PF	8.00
1999 November	.65
1999 November, silver, PF	8.00
1999 December	.70
1999 December, silver, PF	8.00
2000	.75
2000W	5.00
2000 Health	.65
2000 Health, silver, PF	8.00
2000 Freedom	.65
2000 Freedom, silver, PF	6.00
2000 Family	.65
2000 Family, silver, PF	6.00
2000 Community	.65
2000 Community, silver, PF	6.00
2000 Harmony	.65
2000 Harmony, silver, PF	6.00

ELIZABETH II	BU
2000 Wisdom	.65
2000 Wisdom, silver, PF	6.00
2000 Creativity	.65
2000 Creativity, silver, PF	6.00
2000 Ingenuity	.65
2000 Ingenuity, silver, PF	6.00
2000 Achievement	.65
2000 Achievement, silver, PF	6.00
2000 Natural Legacy	.65
2000 Natural Legacy, silver, PF	6.00
2000 Celebration	.65
2000 Celebration, silver, PF	6.00
2000 Pride	.65
2000 Pride, colorized	6.50
2000 Pride, silver, PF	6.00

FIFTY CENTS

Sterling-silver 50-cent pieces were the largest coins struck for domestic circulation from the beginning of Canadian confederation coinage in 1870 until 1912. These coins bore a portrait of an older Queen Victoria. Initial mintages were moderate, and for some time, the government did not replace worn-out coins. So these coins saw hard service. They are more difficult to find in middle to upper grades than one would expect.

With the passing of Queen Victoria, a new portrait was designed for Edward VII in 1902. The first coin struck at the new Canadian mint in 1908 was one of these pieces. There was a bit of a ruckus in 1911 when the new obverse with George V's portrait lacked the Latin phrase Dei Gratia ("by the grace of God"). The mint responded to the public outcry, and beginning in 1912, these titles were added.

As a result of a World War I increase in silver prices, the alloy was reduced from 92.5 percent pure (sterling) to 80 percent beginning with 1920. Most 1921 pieces were melted before they could be released, and no additional 50-cent pieces were struck until 1929. Today, the 1921 50-cent pieces are among the greatest rarities in Canadian coinage.

When the obverse was changed to portray the new King George VI in 1937, the reverse of the 50-cent piece was changed also. Canada's crowned coat of arms was selected, as designed by George Kruger-Gray. This new reverse motif, with significant alterations, continues today.

Because of the time required to modify the royal titles on the dies to reflect the independence of India, some 1947 coins were struck in 1948 with a tiny maple leaf after the date. This variety is not common and quite popular.

No monarch has had as many different portraits on Canadian coins as Elizabeth II. The first portrait, designed by Mary Gillick, had some minor difficulties in striking and, as a result, was subtly modified after production began. In 1965 a new bust wearing a tiara was introduced, years before Britain itself began using it. When a mature head of the queen was desired, the Canadian choice differed from that of Britain. A design with an open crown, by Canadian artist Dora de Pédery-Hunt, was used beginning in 1990. It was replaced in mid-2003 by a bareheaded, grandmotherly portrait designed by Susanna Blunt.

During this reign, the coat of arms on the reverse went through its own evolution. A version with a motto and more elaborate crest was introduced in 1959, only to be modified the next year. The 1959 version was heraldically inaccurate, using the symbol for blue instead of white in the lowest section. In 1997, an additional collar was added around the shield.

As part of a set of wildlife coins struck for the centennial of Canadian independence, the 1967 50-cent piece depicted a howling wolf. Unfortunately, the rising price of silver forced the centennial coins out of circulation. Production of the silver 50-cent piece was suspended, and beginning in 1968, it was reduced in size and produced in pure nickel. It was switched to nickel-plated steel in 2000, with proofs being struck in sterling.

Known Counterfeits: Any 1921 should be examined by an expert.

VICTORIA	VG	VF
1901	55.00	225.00
EDWARD VII	**VG**	**VF**
1902	15.00	100.00
1903H	22.00	175.00
1904	150.00	600.00
1905	150.00	600.00
1906	12.00	95.00
1907	12.00	95.00
1908	21.00	175.00
1909	17.00	175.00
1910, Victorian leaves	22.00	175.00
1910, Edwardian leaves	8.00	85.00

George V 1917 50 Cents

GEORGE V	F	XF
1911	70.00	550.00
1912	24.00	225.00
1913	24.00	300.00
1914	55.00	550.00
1916	14.00	175.00
1917	11.00	100.00
1918	10.00	90.00
1919	10.00	90.00
1920	13.00	125.00
1921	24,000.00	32,000.00
1929	13.00	100.00
1931	29.00	225.00
1932	185.00	800.00
1934	30.00	225.00
1936	29.00	175.00

GEORGE VI	XF	Unc.
1937	10.00	30.00
1938	25.00	90.00
1939	17.00	60.00
1940	6.00	27.00
1941	6.00	27.00
1942	6.00	27.00
1943	6.00	27.00

GEORGE VI	XF	Unc.
1944	6.00	27.00
1945	6.00	30.00
1946	8.00	60.00
1946, hoof in 6	150.00	1,100.00
1947, straight 7	12.00	65.00
1947, curved 7	22.00	100.00
1947, straight 7, maple leaf	70.00	160.00
1947, curved 7, maple leaf	2,200.00	3,900.00
1948	150.00	250.00
1949	7.00	35.00
1949, hoof over 9	60.00	325.00
1950	35.00	125.00
1950, lines in 0	6.00	9.00
1951	—	9.00
1952	—	9.00

George VI 1952 50 Cents

ELIZABETH II	XF	BU
1953, small date, without strap	—	7.00
1953, large date, without strap	14.00	75.00
1953, large date, straps	6.00	22.00
1954	7.00	18.00
1955	6.00	15.00
1956	—	7.00
1957	—	6.00
1958	—	6.00
1959	—	6.50
1960		6.00
1961		6.00
1962		6.00
1963		6.00
1964		6.00
1965		6.00
1966		6.00
1967, centennial		6.00
Nickel		
1968		.65
1969		.65
1970		.65
1971		.65
1972		.65

Elizabeth II 1995 50 Cents

ELIZABETH II	BU
1973	.65
1974	.65
1975	.65
1976	.65
1977	1.35
1978	.65
1979	.65
1980	.65
1981	.65
1982	.65
1983	.65
1984	.65
1985	.65
1986	1.00
1987	1.00
1988	1.00
1989	1.00
1990	1.00
1991	.85
1992, "1867-1992"	.75
1993	.85
1994	.75
1995	.75

ELIZABETH II	BU
1995, puffin, silver, PF	24.00
1995, whooping crane, silver, PF	24.00
1995, gray jays, silver, PF	24.00
1995 ptarmigans, silver, PF	22.00
1996	.65
1996, silver, PF	9.00
1996, moose calf, silver, PF	20.00
1996, wood ducklings, silver, PF	20.00
1996, cougar kittens, silver, PF	20.00
1996, black bear cubs, silver, PF	20.00
1997	.70
1997, silver, PF	10.00
1997, duck tolling retriever, silver, PF	17.00
1997, labrador retriever, silver, PF	17.00
1997, Newfoundland dog, silver, PF	17.00
1997, Eskimo dog, silver, PF	17.00
1998	.70
1998, silver, PF	10.00
1998W, in sets only 2.00	
1998, "1908-1998," silver, PF	15.00
1998, skaters, silver, PF	10.00
1998, ski jumper, silver, PF	10.00
1998, soccer players, silver, PF	10.00

ELIZABETH II	BU
1998, killer whales, silver, PF	17.00
1998, humpback whale, silver, PF	17.00
1998, beluga whales, silver, PF	17.00
1998, blue whale, silver, PF	17.00
1999	.70
1999, silver, PF	10.00
1999P	15.00
1999, golfers, silver, PF	13.50
1999, yacht race, silver, PF	10.00
1999, football, silver, PF	10.00
1999, basketball, silver, PF	9.00
1999, cymric cat, silver, PF	20.00
1999, tonkinese cat, silver, PF	20.00
1999, cougar, silver, PF	20.00
1999, lynx, silver, PF	20.00
2000	1.00
2000, silver, PF	10.00
2000P	3,500.00
2000W, in sets only 1.50	
2000, hockey, silver, PF	12.00
2000, curling, silver, PF	10.00
2000, steeplechase, silver, PF	10.00
2000, bowling, silver, PF	10.00

ELIZABETH II	BU
2000, great horned owl, silver, PF	20.00
2000, red-tailed hawk, silver, PF	20.00
2000, osprey, silver, PF	20.00
2000, bald eagle, silver, PF	20.00

Elizabeth II 1998 50 Cents

DOLLARS

Although patterns were produced as early as 1911, Canada did not issue a silver dollar until 1935. The entire visual style of Canadian coins changed when a new artistic commemorative dollar for the jubilee of George V was released. It depicted the now famous voyageur design of a fur-company agent and Indian paddling a canoe past an islet. This design was retained when the reverses of all other denominations were modernized with the new George VI portrait in 1937.

Because of the time required to modify the royal titles to reflect the independence of India, some 1947 dollars were struck in 1948 with a tiny maple leaf after the date. This variety is scarce and popular. The 1950-52 Arnprior varieties have only 1-1/2 water lines to the right of the canoe, the result of over-polishing of the die.

No monarch has had as many different portraits on Canadian coins as Elizabeth II. The first portrait, designed by Mary Gillick, had some minor difficulties in striking and, as a result, was subtly modified after production began. In 1965 a new bust wearing a tiara was introduced, years before Britain itself began using it. When a mature head of the queen was desired, the Canadian choice differed from that of Britain. A design with an open crown, by Canadian artist Dora de Pédery-Hunt, was used beginning in 1990. It was replaced in mid-2003 by a bareheaded, grandmotherly portrait designed by Susanna Blunt.

The 1967 centennial of Canadian independence was cause for issue of some of the country's most beautiful and dignified wildlife coins. On the dollar, a majestic Canada goose is shown against a stark open background. Unfortunately, the rising price of silver forced these coins out of circulation. Beginning in 1968, the 80-percent-silver dollar was replaced by a smaller one of pure nickel.

In 1987, a radical new dollar coin was introduced to save the expense of producing less-durable paper money. A small golden, bronze-plated nickel dollar depicting a swimming loon was introduced. It was originally intended to use the standard voyageur reverse, but the master dies were temporarily lost in transit. Today, this coin is popularly known as the "loonie."

With its long history as a commemorative, the $1 denomination was a natural for spearheading Canada's modern collector coin program initiated during the 1970s. In most years, a specially cased, silver-alloy dollar is produced for the numismatic market. In many years a base-metal commemo-

GEORGE V	XF	Unc.
1935, silver jubilee	28.00	37.50
1936	26.00	35.00

rative is also issued, available in circulation and collector versions. Cased versions in either silver or base metal should always be kept in their cases of issue. Otherwise, they are considered less salable.

Known Counterfeits: Any 1948 dollar should be examined by an expert.

George V 1935 Dollar

George VI 1939 Dollar

George VI 1951 Dollar

GEORGE VI	XF	Unc.
1937	12.00	25.00
1938	65.00	100.00
1939, royal visit	10.00	12.00
1945	175.00	300.00
1946	35.00	95.00
1947, pointed 7	150.00	265.00
1947, blunt 7	80.00	125.00
1947, maple leaf	175.00	250.00
1948	1,000.00	1,300.00
1949, Newfoundland	16.50	22.50
1950, three water lines	11.00	16.00
1950, Arnprior	21.00	40.00
1951, three water lines	11.00	14.00
1951, Arnprior	60.00	175.00
1952, three water lines	11.00	14.00
1952, Arnprior	22.00	40.00
1952, no water lines	11.00	16.50

Elizabeth II 1958 Dollar

Elizabeth II 1964 Dollar

ELIZABETH II	XF	BU
1953, wire rim, without shoulder strap	—	25.00
1953, flat rim, with shoulder strap	—	25.00
1954	11.00	35.00
1955, three water lines	11.00	30.00
1955, Arnprior	90.00	175.00
1956	13.00	50.00
1957, three water lines	—	16.00
1957, Arnprior	10.00	35.00
1958, British Columbia	—	15.00
1959	—	12.00
1960	—	12.00
1961	—	12.00
1962	—	12.00
1963	—	10.00
1964, Charlottetown	—	10.00
1965	—	10.00
1966	—	11.00
1967, centennial	—	12.00

Nickel (Voyageur reverse through 1987 unless noted.)

1968		1.25
1969		1.25
1970, Manitoba		2.00
1971, British Columbia		2.00

ELIZABETH II	XF	BU
1972	1.50	—
1973, Prince Edward Island	2.00	—
1973, R.C.M.P., silver, proof-like	6.50	—
1974, Winnipeg	2.00	—
1974, Winnipeg, silver, proof-like	7.00	—
1975	1.50	—
1975, Calgary, silver, proof-like	7.00	—
1976	1.50	—
1976, Library of Parliament, silver, proof-like	7.00	—
1977	2.25	—
1977, silver jubilee, silver, proof-like	7.00	—
1978	1.50	—
1978, Commonwealth Games, silver, proof-like	7.00	—
1979	1.50	—
1979, sailing ship, silver, proof-like	8.50	—
1980	1.50	—

ELIZABETH II	BU	PF
1980, Arctic Territories, silver	22.00	—
1981	1.50	—
1981, railroad, silver	8.50	13.50
1982	1.50	5.25
1982, Constitution	3.00	6.00
1982, Regina, silver	8.50	8.50

ELIZABETH II	BU	PF
1983	1.50	5.25
1983, Edmonton Games, silver	8.50	8.50
1984	1.50	6.00
1984, Cartier	2.25	6.00
1984, Toronto, silver	8.50	8.50
1985	1.50	7.00
1985, national parks, silver	8.50	10.00
1986	2.00	7.50
1986, Vancouver, silver	8.50	8.50
1987, in sets only	3.50	7.50
1987, Davis Strait, silver	8.50	9.00

Loon reverse: aureate-bronze plated nickel. Other reverses: silver unless noted. Since 1988, uncirculated commemorative silver dollars have had a proof-like finish.

1987, loon	2.25	8.00
1988, loon	2.25	6.75
1988, Ironworks	8.50	16.00
1989, loon	3.00	6.75
1989, MacKenzie River	14.00	16.00
1990, loon	1.75	7.00
1990, Kelsey	8.50	18.00
1991, loon	1.75	13.00
1991, S.S. Frontenac, silver	8.50	24.00
1992, "1867-1992," loon	2.00	8.00

ELIZABETH II	BU	PF
1992, "1867-1992," Parliament, aureate-bronze plated nickel	2.25	9.00
1992, Stagecoach	16.50	16.50
1993, loon	2.00	6.00
1993, Stanley Cup	16.50	16.50
1994, loon	2.00	7.00
1994, War Memorial, aureate-bronze plated nickel	2.25	7.50
1994, sled dogs	16.50	25.00
1995, loon	3.00	7.00
1995, Peacekeeping Monument, aureate-bronze plated nickel	2.25	7.50
1995, Hudson's Bay Co.	16.50	30.00
1996, loon	2.00	7.50
1996, McIntosh apple	16.50	24.00

Elizabeth II 1997 Dollar

ELIZABETH II	BU	PF
1997, loon, in sets only	5.00	8.00
1997, loon flying, proof-like	—	22.00
1997, loon flying, silver	—	75.00
1997, hockey	16.50	24.00
1998, loon, in sets only	2.50	10.00
1998W, loon, proof-like	—	4.50
1998, R.C.M.P., silver	16.50	20.00
1999, loon, in sets only	2.00	8.00
1999, Year of Old Persons	—	40.00
1999, ship, silver	16.50	22.50
2000, human and space shuttle	16.50	22.50

Elizabeth II 1999 Dollar

EUROPEAN COINS

Modern coinage as we know it began in Europe during the 1500s and spread throughout the world with the establishment of European colonies or the opening of European trade relations. Since this time, coinage manufacture has progressed from hand hammering to screw presses and roller dies and then steam-powered presses. Today's high-tech electronic minting machines, capable of striking thousands of coins a minute, are basically an improved version of the steam-powered presses first used in the late 1700s.

Many people collect European and other world coins by "type." This means one example of each design or one example of each design in each alloy in which it is struck. Others collect one of each date and mintmark, much as U.S. coins are collected. There is no right or wrong way to collect coins. The most important thing is to enjoy the experience and learn by the process. There is no series more extensively documented in catalogs than the coinage of modern Europe, so whatever path the collector chooses, they need not do it in the dark. With the introduction of the euro, the new pan-European currency, people are becoming more aware of the changes in European coinage—past, present and future.

COUNTERFEIT EUROPEAN COINS

Many individual counterfeits are listed under each country, but remember that new counterfeits of more expensive European coins appear every year. This also applies to many more common gold bullion issues.

As a general rule, crown- and thaler-sized coins are more prone to counterfeiting for the collector market. During the 19th and 20th centuries, circulation counterfeits of coins 20 to 28 millimeters were likely to be of tin or lead alloy. Recently, more circulation counterfeits of high-denomination base-metal coins have been reported.

AUSTRIA

Until 1918, the modern coinage of Austria was used in an area much larger than present-day Austria. It circulated in the many lands of the Hapsburg dynasty and their dependent nobles. Modern coin production, using roller dies, began before the reign of Leopold I the Hogmouth (1657-1705), but his later coinage took it to a new height of uniformity. The excellent portraits are perfect examples of the baroque style. Collectors should remember that coins struck with roller dies usually appear slightly curved; this is not a flaw.

The standard design formula is an obverse portrait and a double-headed eagle reverse. It continued through the 1890s, when a crown and values became the most common designs. A few commemoratives were also struck during this time. Austria is one of three modern countries to have used the double-headed eagle. Its coins are easily distinguished because Austria's eagle displays a Hapsburg shield on its breast. Russia's eagle has St. George slaying a dragon on its breast. Serbia's (later Yugoslavia's) eagle has a shield depicting a cross with Cs in the angles. The later Yugoslav shield may be more complex but still contains this element.

After World War I, Austria became a republic and was reduced to its present size. Its circulating coins and commemoratives depict aspects of local history and culture, such as a Royal Lipizzaner stallion, or fauna, such as the edelweiss. During World War II, Austria was aligned with Germany, and Nazi coins with the mintmark "B" were struck in Vienna.

In January 2002, Austria replaced the schilling with coins denominated in euros, the currency of the European Union. On the circulating denominations, 1 cent through 2 euros, one side carries an Austrian design, the other a common European design. On higher-denomination commemoratives, both sides are distinctively Austrian.

During most of Austria's history, powerful nobles and bishops were allowed to strike their own coins. The counts of Tyrol were the most prolific issuers of coins. Their 3-kreuzer coins are particularly common. The archbishops of Salzburg also struck vast numbers of coins at several mints from 996 through 1806.

Known Counterfeits: Most 1915 gold 4-ducat, 1-ducat, 20-corona, and 100-corona coins are modern restrikes.

	VF
1908 2 Heller, eagle (C)	.25
1915 20 Corona (restrike) head of Franz Josef/eagle (G)	190.00

REPUBLIC COINAGE 1923 TO 1938	XF
1924 100 Kronen, eagle head/oak sprig (C)	1.50
1925 Schilling, neo-classical building/shield (S)	3.50
1928 2 Schilling, Schubert/10 shields (S)	5.00
1935 5 Schilling, Madonna and child/eagle (S)	17.50
1926 25 Schilling, eagle (G), proof-like	175.00 Unc.

REPUBLIC COINAGE 1946 TO 2000	Unc.
1972 2 Groschen, eagle (AL)	.50
1946 Schilling, Sower (AL)	20.00
1957 10 Schilling, shield/girl's head (S)	7.50
1974 10 Schilling, eagle/girl's head (CN)	6.00
1996 20 Schilling, Anton Bruckner (ALB)	4.50
1956 25 Schilling, Mozart (S)	8.00
1974 100 Schilling, Olympics (S)	11.00
1982 500 Schilling, printing press (S)	50.00

Austria 1946 Schilling

Austria 1982 500 Schilling

BALKANS

The Ottoman conquest of the Balkan Peninsula ended European-style coinage for most of the region. It was not restored until the 1800s. The only surviving coinages were those of Transylvania and the small Venetian and Ragusan settlements along the Adriatic coast. The former were all copper, the latter a variety of metals.

The first country to regain its independence from the Ottoman Turks was Greece. Its first coinage was distinctive and portrayed the mythological phoenix bird reborn from its ashes, alluding to the rebirth of the Greek nation. After a few years, Greece's coinage took on the less creative forms popular elsewhere in Europe: shields, royal portraits, and a denomination within a wreath. The coinages of the two Greek republics, 1925-1935 and 1974 to date, are also distinctive in their harkening back to ancient times for their inspiration.

Soon Romania (1867), Serbia (1868), Bulgaria (1881), and Montenegro (1906) struck their first modern coinages, on much the same European pattern as mentioned above. Albania lagged behind until 1926. After World War I, Montenegro and the former Austrian territories of Slovenia, Croatia and Bosnia-Herzogovina were joined under the king of Serbia to form Yugoslavia. Following World War II, these kingdoms were all overthrown by communists. Most communist coins follow the typical pattern of a state seal on the obverse and a value or a symbol of agricultural or industrial labor on the reverse. As a result of the Yugoslav civil war, Slovenia, Croatia, Macedonia, and Bosnia-Herzegovina were established as independent states. Moldova came into being as a result of the breakup of the Soviet Union.

Post-communist Balkan coinage varies from monotonous bank monograms to exquisite depictions of flora and fauna. Some of these new governments have even chosen to use the same heraldic motifs found on their coinages during the 1930s. During the last few years, all of these countries have struck collector coins. Some, such as Bosnia's, have been marketed in North America. Others, such as Romania's, have been scantily distributed.

Known Counterfeits: Albanian gold and dollar-sized silver coins of the 1920s and 1930s, particularly the 1938 gold.

ALBANIA	XF
1935 Qindar Ar., eagle (C)	16.00
1926 1/2 Lek, two headed eagle/man fighting lion (N)	15.00
1935 Frang Ar., head of King Zog/arms (S)	24.00
1926 100 Franga Ari., head of Amet Zogu/chariot (G)	1,000.00
1941 .20 Lek, king of Italy in helmet/eagle between fasces (St.)	8.00
1939 10 Lek, king of Italy/similar (S)	120.00
1947 2 Lek, eagle (Z)	3.00
1964 1 Lek, eagle (AL)	2.00
	BU
1988 5 Leke, train/train (CN)	28.00
1996 50 Leke, ancient horseman (CN)	3.00

Albania 1964 Lek

BOSNIA-HERZEGOVINA	BU
1994 500 Dinara, arms over bridge/wolf (CN)	14.00
1998 10 Feninga, triangle/map (copper-plated St.)	.75
2000 2 convertible marks, dove (bimetallic, CN in NB)	15.00

Bosnia-Herzegovina 1998 10 Feninga

BULGARIA	VF
1912 2 Stotinki, arms/wreath (C)	1.00
1925 1 Lev, arms/wreath (CN)	.60
1943 5 Leva, medieval horseman r./wreath (nickel-clad St.)	1.00
1934 100 Leva, head of Boris III/art deco wreath (S)	7.00
Postwar Issues	Unc.
1951 1 Stotinka, arms/grain (B)	.25
1977 50 Stotinki, runner/arms (CN)	2.00
1976 1 Leva, gun and knife/lion (C)	3.00
1979 10 Leva, arms/children (S), PF	25.00
1992 10 Leva, Madara horseman (CN)	2.50
1996 1,000 Leva, sailing ship/wreath (S), PF	36.00

Bulgaria 1979 10 Leva

Croatia 1994 100 Kuna

CROATIA	Unc.
1941 2 Kune, shield (Z)	45.00
1993 1 Lipa, corn (AL)	.50
1994 100 Kuna, St. Blaza church/altar, series II mark (S), PF	50.00
1995 2 Kune, tuna (CN)	2.00
1994 5 Kuna, bear (CN)	4.00
1998 25 Kuna, sailboat (B in CN)	11.50

GREECE	VF
1922 10 Lepta, crown/branch (AL)	2.00
1926 50 Lepta, head of Athena (CN)	1.00
1911 2 Drachmai, head of George/Thetis standing on hippocamp (S)	30.00

	BU
1954 5 Lepta, crowned wreath/wheat (AL, holed)	10.00
1971 50 Lepta, head of Constantine II/Phoenix and soldier (CN)	20.00
1988 1 Drachma, Bouboulina/ship (C)	1.00
1973 20 Drachmai, Phoenix/bust of Athena (CN)	5.00
1964 30 Drachmai, busts of king and queen/double-headed eagle (S)	12.00
1994 50 Drachmes, Kallergis/Parliament (B)	5.00
1996 20,000 Drachmes, olympics (G), PF	500.00

Greece 1996 20,000 Drachmes

GREECE	BU
1998 100 Drachmes, basketball players (B)	6.50
1991 500 Drachmes, cartoon fish/flags (S), PF	75.00
2000 500 Drachmes, woman handing torch to athlete/ olympic symbols (CN)	6.00

Greece 1998 100 Drachmes

MACEDONIA	BU
1993 50 Deni, seagull (B)	1.50
1993 1 Denar, dog (B)	4.00
2000 1 Denar, elaborate cross/Byzantine coin (B)	15.00
1995 2 Denari, fish/FAO symbol (B)	3.50

Macedonia 1993 Denar

MOLDOVA	BU
1993 25 Bani, arms/wreath (AL)	.75
1993 5 Lei, arms (nickel-clad St.)	4.00

MONTENEGRO	VF
1906 2 Pare	12.00
1913 2 Pare, eagle (C)	8.00
1908 20 Para, eagle (N)	7.00
1912 1 Perper, head of Nicholas/arms (S)	14.00
1910 2 Perpera, similar (S)	35.00
1910 10 Perpera, similar (G)	220.00

Moldova 1993 25 Bani

Montenegro 1906 2 Pare

ROMANIA	VF
1921 25 Bani, eagle (AL)	1.50
1939 1 Leu, crown/corn (NB)	.50
1924 2 Lei, arms (CN)	1.75
1930 10 Lei, head of Carol II/eagle (NB)	3.50
1942 20 Lei, crown/wreath (Z)	1.50
1935 250 Lei, head of Carol II/arms on eagle (S)	60.00
1946 2,000 Lei, head of Michael/arms (B)	1.00
1946 100,000 Lei, head of Michael/woman releasing dove (S)	11.50

	Unc.
1952 1 Ban, arms (B)	2.00
1963 5 Bani, arms (N-clad St.)	2.00
1966 3 Lei, arms/factory (N-clad St.)	4.00
1993 1 Leu, arms (C-clad St.)	1.50
1996 10 Lei, arms/sailboat (N-plated St.)	16.00
1993 20 Lei, bust of King Stefan (B-clad St.)	3.00
1999 500 Lei, solar eclipse (AL)	4.00

Romania 1966 3 Lei

SERBIA	VF
1912 5 Para, denomination/arms (CN)	2.00
1915 1 Dinar, head of Peter I/wreath (S)	4.50
1943 10 Dinara, eagle/wreath (Z)	2.50

Serbia 1915 Dinar

SLOVENIA	BU
1992 10 Stotinov, salamander (AL)	.75
1996 50 Stotinov, bee (AL)	.75
1996 5 Tolarjev, locomotive (B)	2.25
1994 500 Tolarjev, quill pen (S), PF	28.50
1993 5,000 Tolarjev, bees around hive (G), PF	225.00
2000 10 Tolarjev, horse (CN)	2.00

Slovenia 2000 10 Tolarjev

YUGOSLAVIA	VF
1925 50 Para, head of Alexander I/wreath (CN)	1.00
1925 1 Dinar, head of Alexander I/wreath (CN)	1.00
1938 2 Dinara, crown (ALB)	1.00
1932 50 Dinara, head of Alexander I/eagle (S)	22.00
1945 Dinar, arms (Z)	1.00
1953 50 Para, arms (AL)	.50
1981 10 Dinara, arms (CN)	1.25
	Unc.
1981 10 Dinara, arms (CN)	1.25
1983 500 Dinara, Olympic symbols/ski jumper (S), PF	14.00
1980 1,000 Dinara, Vukovar Congress (S), PF	27.50
1990 1 Dinar, arms (CNZ)	.25
1992 1 Dinar, bank monogram (B)	.60
1993 10 Dinara, bank monogram (CNZ)	.70
1996 1 New Dinar, eagle shield (CNZ)	1.00
1996 20 New Dinar, eagle shield/bust of Nikola Tesla (CNZ), PF	12.50

Yugoslavia 1938 2 Dinara

Yugoslavia 1953 50 Para

Yugoslavia 1992 Dinar

Yugoslavia 1993 10 Dinara

BALTIC STATES

The regions that today are Estonia, Latvia, Lithuania, and Finland were submerged under the domination of Russia, Poland, Germany, and Sweden in various combinations until 1918. Usually these greater powers permitted certain cities, such as Riga, or certain nobles to strike coins. These were somewhat common in the 1600s, but by the 1700s, they ceased to be significant. During the 1800s, these states were not permitted to strike their own coinage except for Finland, which was a semiautonomous grand duchy under Russia.

The collapse of the great European empires during World War I liberated these countries from Russia, the most recent power to dominate the area. The coats of arms of these newly independent states were used on one side or the other of virtually every coin struck between the wars. In most cases, the other side was a monotonous indication of value, but certain other pieces were exceptionally attractive. Most notable are beautiful renditions of the personification of Latvia. Lithuania also struck interesting commemoratives.

Except for Finland, all of these countries were conquered by the Soviet Union in 1940. They re-emerged with the breakup of the Soviet empire in 1989. It is almost shocking how closely some of the new post-Soviet Baltic coins resemble the coins struck by these countries in the 1930s. The exception, of course, is Finland, whose coinage could evolve during its longer independence. Since

1951, its modernistic commemoratives have been released in quantity to the world collector market.

In January 2002, Finland replaced the markka with coins denominated in euros, the currency of the European Union. Some coins were struck years in advance and held until 2002. On the circulating denominations, 1 cent through 2 euros, one side carries a Finnish design, the other a common European design. On higher-denomination commemoratives, both sides are distinctively Finnish.

Known Counterfeits: 1951 500 Markkaa and possibly the 1918 Red Government 5 penniä.

ESTONIA	VF
1922 3 Marka, three lions (CN)	7.00
1926 5 Marka, shield in wreath (CN)	170.00
1929 1 Sent, three lions/oak leaves (C)	3.00
1935 20 Senti, shield (CN)	8.00
1934 1 Kroon, shield in wreath/Viking ship (ALB)	10.00
1930 2 Krooni, shield in wreath/castle (S)	12.00
1932 2 Krooni, shield in wreath/university building (S)	30.00
1991 5 Senti, three lions (B)	.30 Unc.
	BU
1993 5 Krooni, doe (B)	7.00
1992 100 Krooni, three lions/three swallows (S), PF	45.00
1998 100 Krooni, man on eagle head (S), PF	50.00

Estonia 1998 100 Krooni

FINLAND	VF
1913 1 Penni, crowned NII (C)	.65
1917 25 Penniä, Russian eagle (S)	.75
	XF
1917 25 Penniä, eagle without crown, (civil-war issue) (S)	.50
1918 5 Penniä, trumpets (C)	45.00
	Unc.
1919 1 Penni, lion (C)	1.75
1943 10 Penniä, rosette, holed (C)	2.50
1986 50 Penniä, lion/tree (ALB)	1.00
1993 10 Markkaa, Capercaille bird/branches (B center, CN ring)	3.50
1956 100 Markkaa, shield/trees (S)	3.00
1990 100 Markkaa, lyre/owl (S)	40.00
1952 500 Markkaa, Olympic rings/wreath (S)	50.00
1999 2 Euro Cent, lion/globe (C-plated St.)	1.25

Finland 1943 10 Penniä

Finland 1990 100 Markkaa

LATVIA	VF
1935 1 Santims, shield (C)	4.00
1939 2 Santimi, shield (C)	5.00
1922 5 Santimi, shield (C)	4.00
1922 10 Santimu, shield (N)	3.00
1922 50 Santimu, shield/Latvia gazing from rudder of ship (N)	7.00
1924 1 Lats, shield/wreath (S)	10.00
1925 2 Lati, similar (S)	10.00
1931 5 Lati, head of Latvia r/arms (S)	25.00
Restored Republic	**BU**
1992 2 Santimi, shield (C-plated St.)	2.00
1992 1 Lats, arms/fish (CN)	7.00
1992 2 Lati, arms/cow (CN)	9.00
1995 10 Latu, arms/schooner (S), PF	50.00
1998 100 Latu, arms/logo (G), PF	525.00

Latvia 1922 10 Santimu

LITHUANIA	VF
1936 1 Centas, knight riding l. (C)	10.00
1936 2 Centai, similar (C)	15.00
1925 10 Centu, knight riding l./ear of grain (ALB)	15.00
1925 50 Centu, similar (ALB)	20.00
1925 1 Litas, similar/oak branch (S)	10.00
1925 2 Litu, similar/wreath (S)	10.00
1925 5 Litai, similar (S)	20.00
1936 5 Litai, similar/bust l. (S)	12.00
1938 10 Litu, stylized castle/bust l. (S)	50.00
Restored Republic	**Unc.**
1991 5 Centai, knight riding l. (AL)	.30
1997 50 Centu, similar (B)	1.00
1997 1 Litas, bust/knight riding l. (CN)	15.00
1994 10 Litu, two harps/similar (CN), PF	20.00
1996 50 Litu, basketball players/shield (S), PF	60.00

Lithuania 1996 50 Litu

BRITISH ISLES

Despite successful experiments with milled (screw-press) coinage during the reign of Elizabeth I (1558-1603), this means of striking uniform, well-made coins was not adopted in England until 1663, after the restoration of the monarchy. By this time, there were many different denominations in silver, from the tiny penny to the crown (60 pence), which had finally become common.

By the end of the century, most of the silver denominations below 6 pence were struck only for ceremonial distribution on Maundy Thursday, the Thursday before Easter. These silver coins were given to the poor but usually passed into circulation. After the mid-1700s, their value as collectibles was so established that almost all were immediately sold by their recipients to collectors and today survive in high grade.

Another change was the replacement of puny, privately made royal contract farthings with officially struck regal farthings and halfpennies of good weight. For a while, the government replaced these coppers with ones of tin, but this was soon abandoned because of their tendency to corrode.

The designs on British coins have usually been conservative. The shield on a cross used before the Civil War was continued after it. New designs were often heraldic as well, sometimes showing one shield, other times showing arrangements of the shields of England, Scotland, Ireland, and France. (England claimed France until the early 1800s.) The new copper coins show a seated female, Britannia, an allegory for Britain dating back to Roman days.

During the 1700s, the government failed to provide enough coins to satisfy Britain's growing industrial economy. The Industrial Revolution also provided the answer to this dilemma. Merchants and miners took matters into their own hands and contracted with modern factories to strike their own money. These tokens, common from the late 1780s and 1790s as well as from 1811 to 1815, depict a delightful array of scenes, from Gothic cathedrals to the machines of the Industrial Revolution.

Gradually the government responded. New steam-power-struck coppers were introduced in 1797-99, including the first penny to be struck in copper instead of silver. A massive issue of machine-struck silver and gold was released in 1816. Notable is the powerful baroque-style depiction of St. George slaying the dragon by Benedetto Pistrucci, used on the crown and gold pieces.

During Queen Victoria's reign (1837-1901), old designs were sometimes given a beautiful neo-Gothic interpretation. Another innovation on the practical side was the replacement of the copper coins with slightly smaller bronze coins. These wore much better than coins of pure copper.

The two world wars took their toll on British coinage. The purity of the silver was lowered from 92.5 percent to 50 percent in 1920 after World War I. Silver was replaced completely by cupro-nickel after World War II in 1947. From the Great Depression onward, gold ceased to circulate. The gold sovereigns struck from then until today were solely for bullion or collector purposes.

After 1,100 years of using a coinage derived from the penny of Charlemagne and based on multiples of 12, Britain finally replaced the pound of 240 pence with a decimal new pence. The new seven-sided 50 pence introduced in 1969 proved so popular that since then, many countries have used this shape for their coinage.

During the second half of the 20th century, collector commemoratives were issued frequently. From the 1970s onward, new creative designs were used for these coins. Many were sold at a premium and were never placed in circulation.

IRELAND

Irish coins continued longer but were usually limited to base metal. From the restoration until 1823, Ireland was usually provided with distinctive halfpennies, farthings, and ultimately pennies with a crowned harp on their reverses. The first machine-made coins were struck in 1805. There were two important exceptions. After James II was forced to flee England in 1688, he managed to hold on to Ireland for several months. To help finance his war to keep the throne, he struck high-value coins in brass containing metal from melted cannons. These 6 pences, shillings, half crowns, and crowns were dated to the month and are called "gun money." Another exception came from 1804-13 when the Bank of Ireland struck silver 5, 10, and 30 pence and 6-shilling tokens to ease the coinage shortage. Ireland's first independent coinage was introduced in 1928.

THE EMPIRE & COMMONWEALTH

Colonial coins struck during the 1700s and early 1800s, less common than the later ones, were similar in style to British issues. Coins struck for the 13 colonies in America are discussed in the book *Warman's U.S. Coins & Currency Field Guide, 3rd Edition*. One big exception are the coins of the East India Co. Many of these are hardly distinguishable from local Indian states and Mogul Empire coins. Usually they are identified by certain symbols or their machine-made fabric, but they were originally intended to circulate alongside local coins, and their designs made this possible.

During the mid-1800s, colonial coins became increasingly more practical in their designs, and many have no motif other than a large number indicating the value. Beginning in the 1920s in most territories, somewhat earlier in a few others, local color and creativity entered into colonial coin design. Native plants and animals were depicted. Some larger values bore the individual colony's coat of arms. Many of the designs were so pleasing that they continued in use for decades, even after independence. As in the homeland, silver was phased out after World War II.

Many independent former colonies still recognize the British monarch. These British Commonwealth members often voluntarily depict the monarch on the obverses of their coins, as they did before independence. Most are listed here for convenience, except Canada, which is covered in depth in its own section.

Known Counterfeits: Circulation counterfeits include the 1916 shilling and the 1900, 1918 and 1942 florin.

A great many sovereigns have been counterfeited, many originating in Lebanon. Some known examples include the 1910, 1911, 1913, 1918M, 1923SA (altered date), and 1927SA. Some were even found in lots bought in the Middle East to issue to British troops during the first Gulf War. Despite their commonness, all sovereigns should be examined carefully.

Recently, base-metal counterfeits of British trade dollars have been seen in abundance. Collector counterfeits have been made of many coins with rare dates spanning the last 150 years, including the 1905 half crown.

GREAT BRITAIN

Victoria, 1901	VF
1901 Farthing, head l./Britannia seated (C)	.75
1901 Penny, similar (C)	1.50
1901 Shilling, head l./crowned shields (S)	10.00
1901 Half Crown, head l./shield (S)	27.00
Edward VII, 1901-10	**VF**
1903 Farthing, head r./Britannia seated (C)	1.50
1910 3 Pence, head r./crowned 3 (S)	1.50
1910 6 Pence, head r./crown (S)	8.50
1910 Florin, head r./Britannia standing (S)	20.00
1902 Crown, head r./ St. George slaying dragon (S)	75.00
1910 Sovereign, similar (G)	215.00

George V, 1910-36	VF
1917 Farthing, head l./Britannia seated (C)	.35
1928 Halfpenny, similar (C)	.50
1935 Penny, similar (C)	.50
1929 Sixpence, head l./six acorns (S)	2.00
1926 Shilling, head l./lion on crown (S)	3.50
1928 Florin, head l./cross of shields, scepters in angles (S)	3.00
1935 Half Crown, head l./shield (S)	5.00
1935 Crown, head l./St. George armored, slaying dragon (S)	15.00
1911 Half Sovereign, similar but saint nude (G)	110.00
1932 Maundy set: 1, 2, 3, 4 Pence, head l./crown over value (S)	185.00 Unc.
George VI, 1936-52	VF
1940 Farthing, head l./wren (C)	.25
1943 Farthing, head l./wren (C)	.15
1942 Halfpenny, head l./ship (C)	.20
1944 Penny, head l./Britannia seated (C)	.50
1937 3 Pence, head l./thrift plant (NB)	.40
1946 Sixpence, head l./crowned GRI (S)	.60
1943 Shilling, head l./Scottish crest (lion standing on crown) (S)	1.25
1950 Half Crown, head l./shield (CN)	.50
1951 Crown, head l./St. George slaying dragon (CN), proof-like	22.50

Elizabeth II, 1952-	Unc.
1954 Farthing, young bust/wren	5.00
1962 Penny, young bust/Britannia seated (C)	1.00
1967 Penny, similar	.30
1966 3 Pence, young bust/Portcullis (castle gate) (NB)	.50
1963 Shilling, young bust/crowned shield (CN)	1.25
1967 Florin, young bust/rose within border (CN)	2.00
1965 Crown, young bust/bust of Churchill (CN)	2.00
1958 Sovereign, young bust/St. George slaying dragon (G)	245.00

Great Britain 1935 Half Crown

Great Britain 1940 Farthing

Great Britain 1943 Schilling

Great Britain 1967 Penny

Decimal Coinage	Unc.
1971 1 New Penny, bust in tiara/portcullis (C)	.20
1987 5 Pence, bust in crown/crowned thistle (CN)	.30
1990 20 Pence, bust in crown/crowned rose (CN, heptagonal)	.75
1981 25 New Pence, bust in tiara/heads of Charles and Diana (CN)	2.50
1973 50 New Pence, bust in tiara/wreath of hands (CN, heptagonal)	2.50
2000 50 Pence, older head in tiara/Britannia (CN, heptagonal)	1.75
2000 50 Pence, older head in tiara/book and library (CN, heptagonal)	2.75
1995 Pound, bust in tiara/Welsh dragon (NB)	5.50
1988 50 Pounds, bust in tiara/Britannia standing (G, two ounces)	510.00

IRELAND (Irish Free State)	VF
1928 Farthing, harp/woodcock (C)	1.50
1935 Penny, harp/hen and chicks (C)	1.00
1937 Penny, similar	1.00
1928 6 Pence, harp/wolfhound (N)	1.00
1928 Shilling, harp/bull (S)	5.00
1928 Florin, harp/salmon (S)	7.00

Irish Free State 1937 Penny

Irish Republic	XF
1953 Halfpenny, harp/pig and piglets (C)	.25
1964 3 Pence, harp/hare (CN)	.50
1939 Shilling, harp/bull (S)	12.50
1962 Shilling, similar (CN)	1.00
1963 Half Crown, harp/horse (CN)	2.00
1966 10 Shillings, bust of Pearse/statue of Cuchulainn (S)	15.00

Irish Republic 1964 3 Pence

Decimal Coinage	BU
1971 Penny, harp/Celtic bird (C)	.75
1986 20 Pence, harp/horse (B)	4.00
1988 50 Pence, harp/arms of Dublin (CN)	3.50
1990 Pound, harp/stag (CN)	8.00

Irish Republic 1971 Penny

BRITISH COLONIES & COMMONWEALTH

AUSTRALIA	VF
1927 Halfpenny, bust of George V (C)	1.00
1949 Penny, head of George VI/kangaroo (C)	.25
1910 3 Pence, bust of Edward VII/arms (S)	7.00
1936 6 Pence, bust of George V/arms (S)	3.00
1943 6 Pence, head of George VI/arms (S)	1.75
1942 Shilling, similar/ram's head (S)	3.00
1910 Florin, bust of Edward VII/arms (S)	150.00
1927 Florin, bust of George V/Parliament (S)	7.00
1937 Crown, head of George VI/crown (S)	17.50
1918 Sovereign, head of George V/St. George slaying dragon (G)	220.00
Elizabeth II	**XF**
1961 Penny, young bust/kangaroo (C)	.20
1964 3 Pence, young head/wheat (S)	.50
1954 6 Pence, young bust/arms (S)	1.75
1961 Shilling, young bust/ram's head (S)	1.25
1960 Florin, young bust/arms (S)	3.75

Decimal Coinage	BU
1981 1 Cent, bust in tiara/ring-tailed opossum	.40
1966 2 Cents, bust in tiara/frilled lizard (C)	1.00
1966 50 Cents, bust in tiara/arms (S)	8.50
1988 2 Dollars, bust in crown/aboriginal man (ALB)	5.00
1993 2 Dollars, bust in crown/kookabura r. (S, two ounces)	125.00
1996 5 Dollars, similar/bust of Donald Bradman (bimetallic, ALB in St.)	12.50
1999 30 Dollars, bust in tiara/rabbit r. (S, 1 kilo)	650.00
1995 40 Dollars, bust in crown/emu (palladium)	500.00

Australia 1937 Crown

Australia 1966 50 Cents

Australia 1993 2 Dollars

BAHAMAS	BU
1971 1 Cent, starfish (C)	2.00
1966 10 Cents, two fish (CN, scalloped)	1.50
1974 15 Cents, hibiscus (CN)	1.50
1972 25 Cents, sloop (N)	1.50
1966 1 Dollar, conch shell (S)	11.00
1971 2 Dollars, two flamingos (S)	20.00
1967 20 Dollars, lighthouse (G)	250.00

Bahamas 1972 2 Dollars

BARBADOS	BU
1973 Cent, arms (C)	.75
ND (1976) 5 Cents, arms/lighthouse (B)	3.00
1970 4 Dollars, arms/sugar cane, banana tree branch (CN)	20.00
1984 5 Dollars, arms/shell fountain (CN)	7.50
1996 5 Dollars, arms/royal couple (S), PF	40.00
1986 25 Dollars, arms/discus thrower (S), PF	30.00

Barbados 1986 25 Dollars

BELIZE	BU
1973 1 Cent, crowned bust (C)	.60
1979 50 Cents, similar (CN)	4.50
1990 1 Dollar, bust in tiara/Columbus' ships (NB, decagonal)	3.00
1990 2 Dollars, similar/EE monogram (CN)	7.50

Belize 1990 2 Dollars

BERMUDA	BU
1964 Crown, crowned bust/arms (S)	10.00
1970 1 Cent, bust in tiara/boar (C)	.50
1996 2 Dollars, crowned bust/horse carriage (S), PF	35.00
1996 60 Dollars, bust in tiara/map above ship (G, curved triangle), PF	1,000.00

BRITISH CARIBBEAN TERRITORIES	BU
1964 1 Cent, crowned bust/wreath (C)	.35
1956 5 Cents, similar/ship (B)	1.00
1964 10 Cents, similar/ship (CN)	.65
1955 50 Cents, similar/queen standing over arms of islands (CN)	3.50

Bermuda 1996 2 Dollars

BRITISH GUIANA	VF
1936 4 Pence, bust of George V/similar (S)	2.50
1945 4 Pence, head of George VI/similar (S)	1.75

BRITISH HONDURAS	VF
1972 1 Cent, head of Elizabeth II (C, scalloped)	.10
1907 5 Cents, bust of Edward VII (CN)	50.00
1936 10 Cents, bust of George V (S)	12.00
1952 25 Cents, head of George VI	5.00
1964 50 Cents, bust of Elizabeth II (CN)	.50

The above are usually found worn.

British Honduras 1972 Cent

BRITISH NORTH BORNEO	VF
1928 5 Cents, arms (CN)	8.00

British North Borneo 1928 5 Cents

BRITISH VIRGIN ISLANDS	BU
1983 10 Cents, bust in tiara/kingfisher (CN)	2.50
1973 25 Cents, similar/cuckoo (CN)	1.75
1985 20 Dollars, similar/Spanish colonial cob coin (S), PF	15.00
1975 100 Dollars, similar/tern (G)	200.00

British Virgin Islands 1985 20 Dollars

BRITISH WEST AFRICA	VF
1908 1/10 Penny, titles of Edward VII/six-pointed star (AL)	3.00
1908 similar (CN)	.50
1920 Penny, titles of George V/six-pointed star (CN)	2.00
1936 Penny, titles of Edward VIII/similar (CN)	1.00
1956 Penny, titles of Elizabeth II/similar (C)	.60
1940 3 Pence, head of George VI/wreath (B)	.60
1913 6 Pence, bust of George V/wreath (S)	5.00
1938 Shilling, head of George VI/palm tree (NB)	1.25
1938 2 Shillings, similar (NB)	2.00

British West Africa 1908 1/10 Penny

CAYMAN ISLANDS	BU
1972 10 Cents, Elizabeth II/green turtle (CN)	1.00
1992 1 Dollar, Elizabeth II/iguana (S), PF	50.00
1975 100 Dollars, Elizabeth II/five queens (G)	360.00

Cayman Islands 1975 100 Dollars

CEYLON	VF
1957 2 Cents, Elizabeth II (B, scalloped)	.15
1910 5 Cents, bust of Edward VII (CN, square)	2.00
1911 25 Cents, George V/palm tree (S)	6.00
1929 50 Cents, bust of George V/palm tree (S)	5.00
1951 50 Cents, head of George VI (NB)	.35
1940 3 Pence, head of George VI/wreath (B)	.60
CYPRUS	VF
1908 1/2 Piastre, Edward VII (C)	200.00
1931 1 Piastre, George V (C)	50.00
1934 1 Piastre, similar, (CN, scalloped)	2.50
1901 3 Piastres, bust of Victoria/crowned 3 (S)	25.00
1921 9 Piastres, bust of George V/crowned shield (S)	10.00
1947 Shilling, head of George VI/two lions (CN)	4.00
	Unc.
1955 3 Mils, bust of Elizabeth II/fish (C)	.25
1974 5 Mils, arms/ship (C)	.35
1955 50 Mils, similar/ferns (CN)	1.00

Cyprus 1974 5 Mils

EAST AFRICA	VF
1908 1/2 Cent, titles of Edward VII/tusks (AL)	25.00
1923 1 Cent, titles of George V/tusks (C)	.50
1956 1 Cent, titles of Elizabeth II/tusks (C)	.20
1936 5 Cents, titles of Edward VIII/tusks (C)	.50
1913 25 Cents, bust of George V/lion (S)	10.00
1963 50 Cents, bust of Elizabeth II/lion (CN)	.25
1946 Shilling, head of George VI/lion (billon)	2.00

East Africa 1913 25 Cents

EAST CARIBBEAN STATES	BU
1981 1 Cent, bust in tiara/wreath (AL)	.30
1989 1 Dollar, similar/ship (CN, 10-sided)	3.25
1994 10 Dollars, mature bust/soccer ball and Manhattan buildings (S), PF	45.00
1996 10 Dollars, similar/yacht (S), PF	50.00

East Caribbean States 1994 10 Dollars

FIJI	VF
1934 Halfpenny, titles of George V (CN, holed)	1.75
1936 Penny, titles of Edward VIII (CN, holed)	1.00
1950 3 Pence, head of George VI/hut (B)	1.00
1965 6 Pence, bust of Elizabeth II/sea turtle (CN)	.30
1934 Shilling, bust of George V/outrigger (S)	4.00
1943 Florin, head of George VI/shield (S)	6.00

	BU
1976 1 Cent, bust of Elizabeth II/dish (C)	1.00
1992 1 Cent, bust of Elizabeth II/dish (C)	.75
1987 50 Cents, similar/sailing canoe (CN, 12-sided)	4.00
1995 1 Dollar, similar/drinking vessel (B)	3.50
1986 10 Dollars, similar/Fijian ground frog (S), PF	25.00
1996 10 Dollars, similar/dancer (S), PF	17.50
1978 250 Dollars, similar/banded iguana (G)	975.00

Fiji 1992 Cent

Fiji 1996 10 Dollars

GIBRALTAR	BU
1967 Crown, bust of Elizabeth II/castle (CN)	6.00
1988 5 Pence, similar/Barbary ape (CN)	1.50
1990 50 Pence, similar/five dolphins (CN, seven-sided)	7.00
1996 Crown, similar/Audrey Hepburn (CN)	9.50
1989 5 Sovereigns, similar/Una and lion (G), PF	1,150.00
2000 1 Crown, similar/jumper and kangaroo (CN)	10.00

Gibraltar 2000 Crown

GUERNSEY	VF
1903 Double, shield (C)	.50
1929 2 Doubles, shield (C)	1.25
	BU
1959 8 Doubles, shield/three lilies (C)	2.50
1966 10 Shillings, Elizabeth II/William the Conqueror (CN, square)	2.00
1971 2 New Pence, shield/windmill (C)	.50
1983 Pound, shield/sailing ship (NB)	4.50
1994 25 Pounds, Elizabeth II/Normandy invasion (G)	245.00
1996 5 Pounds, Elizabeth II/Elizabeth the Queen Mother (S), PF	45.00

Guernsey 1996 5 Pounds

HONG KONG	VF
1905 1 Cent, Edward VII/Chinese inscription (C)	7.50
1932 5 Cents, George V/similar (S)	1.50
1937 5 Cents, George VI/similar (N)	1.25
1948 10 Cents, George VI/similar (NB)	.50
1902 20 Cents, Edward VII/similar (S)	40.00
1996 5 Pounds, Elizabeth II/Elizabeth the Queen Mother (S), PF	45.00
	BU
1975 20 Cents, Elizabeth II/similar (B)	.50
1960 1 Dollar, Elizabeth II/lion (CN)	6.00
1993 2 Dollars, Bauhinia flower (CN, scalloped)	1.50
1994 10 Dollars, similar (B in CN)	6.00
1977 1,000 Dollars, Elizabeth II/snake (G)	475.00
1987 1,000 Dollars, Elizabeth II/rabbit (G)	475.00

Hong Kong 1937 5 Cents

Hong Kong 1960 Dollar

INDIA—REGAL COINAGE	VF
1906 1/12th Anna, Edward VII/wreath (C)	1.00
1916 1/12th Anna, George V/wreath (C)	.50
1939 1/12th Anna, George VI/wreath (C)	.50
1906 1/4 Anna, Edward VII/wreath (C)	1.75
1920 1/4 Anna, George V/wreath (C)	.40
1942 1/4 Anna, George VI/wreath (C)	.50
1943 1 Pice, Crown/wreath (C)	.50
1946 1/2 Anna, George VI (CN)	.25
1936 1 Anna, George V (CN)	.35
1945 1 Anna, George VI (NB)	.25
1901 2 Annas, Victoria as empress/wreath (S)	2.50
1918 2 Annas, George V (CN, square)	1.75
1940 2 Annas, George VI (CN, square)	.30
1919 4 Annas, George V (CN)	5.00
1904 1/4 Rupee, Edward VII/flowers (S)	3.50
1936 1/4 Rupee, George V/wreath (S)	2.50
1945 1/4 Rupee, George VI/wreath (S)	1.50
1946 1/4 Rupee, George VI/tiger (N)	.75
1919 8 Annas, George V (CN)	7.50
1903 Rupee, Edward VII/flowers (S)	9.00
1914 Rupee, George V/wreath (S)	8.00
1945 Rupee, George VI/wreath (S)	3.50
1947 Rupee, George VI/tiger (N)	2.50

INDIA—REGAL COINAGE	VF
1918 15 Rupees, George V/wreath (G)	350.00
1918 Sovereign, George V/St. George slaying dragon, mintmark "I" on ground (G)	215.00

INDIA—PRINCELY STATES	VF
Bharatpur, 1910 VS (1858) Rupee, Victoria/Arabic inscription (S)	85.00
Bundi, 1989 VS (1932) Rupee, Emperor George V, dagger/Hindi inscription (S)	10.00
Kutch, 1936 5 Kori, titles of Edward VIII (S)	7.00
1943 1/8 Kori, titles of George VI (C, holed)	.40
Sailana, 1912 1/4 Anna, George V/inscription (C)	5.00

India-Regal Coinage 1946 1/2 Anna

India-Regal Coinage 1946 1/4 Rupee

ISLE OF MAN	BU
1971 1 New Penny, Elizabeth II/Celtic cross (C)	.65
1980 10 Pence, Elizabeth II/falcon (CN)	2.00
1990 1/5 Crown, Elizabeth II/alley cat (G)	195.00
1976 Crown, Elizabeth II/George Washington (CN)	7.00
same (S)	17.50
1983 Crown, Elizabeth II/1783 balloon (CN)	10.00
1988 Crown, Elizabeth II/Manx cat (S), PF	20.00
1985 1 Angel, Elizabeth II/Archangel Michael slaying demon (G, one ounce)	925.00
2000 1 Crown, Elizabeth II/Willem Barents (CN)	8.00

Isle of Man 1976 Crown

Isle of Man 1988 Crown

JAMAICA	VF
1928 Farthing, George V/shield (CN)	2.00
1950 Farthing, George VI/shield (NB)	.25
1907 Halfpenny, Edward VII/shield (CN)	3.00
1937 Halfpenny (NB)	1.00
1940 Halfpenny, George VI/shield (NB)	.75
1910 Penny, Edward VII/shield (CN)	2.50
1920 Penny, George V/shield (CN)	2.50
1937 Penny, George VI in high relief/shield (NB)	1.75
1950 Penny, George VI in low relief/shield (NB)	.35
1953 Penny (NB)	.20
1958 Penny, Elizabeth II/arms (NB)	.20
	BU
1964 Halfpenny, Elizabeth II/arms (NB)	1.00
1966 5 Shillings, crown in chain/arms (CN)	6.50

Jamaica 1937 Halfpenny

Jamaica 1953 Penny

JERSEY	VF
1909 1/24 Shilling, Edward VII/shield (C)	2.50
1937 1/24 Shilling, George VI/shield (C)	1.00
1931 1/12 Shilling, George V/shield (C)	1.25
	BU
1964 1/12 Shilling, Elizabeth II/shield (C)	2.00
1981 Penny, Elizabeth II/shield (C)	.25
1983 10 Pence, Elizabeth II/prehistoric stone structure (CN)	1.50
1972 2 Pounds 50 Pence, Elizabeth II/lobster (S)	18.00

Jersey 1909 1/24 Shilling

Jersey 1931 1/12 Shilling

MALAYA	VF
1943 1 Cent, George VI (C, square)	.50
1958 1 Cent, Elizabeth II (C, square)	.10

Malaya 1958 Cent

MAURITIUS	VF
1969 1 Cent, Elizabeth II (C)	.10
1949 2 Cents, George VI (C)	1.25
1917 5 Cents, George V (C)	24.50
1975 1/4 Rupee, Elizabeth II/crown and flowers (CN)	.30
1950 1/2 Rupee, George VI/stag (CN)	1.00
1934 1 Rupee, George V/shield (S)	10.00
1975 25 Rupees, Elizabeth II/butterfly (S)	28.00 BU

Mauritius 1934 Rupee

Mauritius 1949 2 Cents

Mauritius 1975 25 Rupees

NEW GUINEA	XF
1929 1/2 Penny, crown and scepters (CN, holed)	275.00
1936 Penny, crown and ERI (C, holed)	2.50
1944 Penny, crown and GRI (C, holed)	6.00
1944 3 Pence, similar (CN, holed)	8.50
1935 Shilling, titles of George V, crown and scepters (S, holed)	3.75
1938 Shilling, similar but George VI (S, holed)	3.75

New Guinea 1929 1/2 Penny

New Guinea 1938 Shilling

NEW ZEALAND	VF
1940 Halfpenny, George VI/Tiki idol (C)	.50
1950 Penny, George VI/Tui bird (C)	.40
1933 3 Pence, George V/crossed clubs (S)	3.00
1952 3 Pence, George VI/similar (CN)	.75
1943 6 Pence, George VI/Huia bird (S)	7.00
1952 Shilling, George VI/Maori warrior (CN)	10.00
1935 Florin, George V/Kiwi bird (S)	30.00
1943 Half Crown, George VI/arms (S)	15.00
1951 Half Crown, similar (CN)	2.50
1935 Crown, George V/Maori chief and British naval officer shaking hands (S)	2,000.00
	BU
1949 Crown, George VI/fern leaf (S)	40.00
1965 Halfpenny, Elizabeth II wearing wreath/Tiki idol (C)	2.50
1965 Penny, similar/Tui bird (C)	6.00
1960 3 Pence, Elizabeth II/crossed clubs (CN)	2.00
1956 6 Pence, similar/Huia bird (S)	22.50
1964 Shilling, similar/Maori warrior (CN)	2.00
1965 Florin, similar/Kiwi bird (CN)	1.50
1953 Crown, similar/crowned monogram (CN)	12.50
1987 1 Cent, crowned bust of Elizabeth II/fern leaf (C)	1.00
1967 2 Cents, bust of Elizabeth II wearing tiara/Kowhai plant (C)	.25
1967 5 Cents, bust of Elizabeth II wearing tiara/Tuatata lizard (CN)	.50

NEW ZEALAND	BU
1988 10 Cents, similar/Maori mask (CN)	1.00
1993 50 Cents, similar/H.M.S. Endeavor (CN)	5.00
1994 50 Cents, similar (ALB in CN)	20.00
1967 Dollar, bust of Elizabeth II wearing tiara/shield between branches (CN)	1.25
1990 Dollar, similar/Kiwi bird (ALB)	5.00
1999 2 Dollars, similar/heron (ALB)	5.00
1996 5 Dollars, similar/Kaka parrot (CN)	25.00
similar (S), PF	30.00

New Zealand 1949 Crown

New Zealand 1951 Half Crown

New Zealand 1967 2 Cents

New Zealand 1990 Dollar

New Zealand 1999 2 Dollars

NIGERIA	BU
1959 1/2 Penny, crown/six-pointed star (C)	1.25
1962 Shilling, Elizabeth II/palm branches (CN)	4.00
1959 2 Shillings, Elizabeth II/peanut plant (CN)	7.00

Nigeria 1959 2 Shillings

RHODESIA	BU
1974 1 Cent, arms (C)	1.25
1964 6 Pence = 5 Cents, Elizabeth II wearing tiara/flame lily (CN)	1.50
1964 2 Shillings = 20 Cents, similar/ancient bird sculpture (CN)	3.25
1966 Pound, similar/lion holding tusk (G), PF	250.00

Rhodesia 1974 Cent

RHODESIA & NYASALAND	BU
1964 Half Penny, giraffes (C, holed)	6.00
1957 1 Shilling, Elizabeth II/antelope (CN)	10.00
1957 2 Shillings, Elizabeth II/African fish eagle holding fish (CN)	15.00

Rhodesia & Nyasaland 1957 Shilling

SEYCHELLES	VF
1948 2 Cents, George VI (C)	.35
1944 25 Cents, similar (S)	3.50
	BU
1959 2 Cents, Elizabeth II (C)	3.00
1972 5 Cents, Elizabeth II/cabbage (AL)	.50
1974 1/2 Rupee, Elizabeth II (CN)	1.50
1972 5 Rupees, Elizabeth II/beach scene with tree and turtle (CN)	6.00
similar (S), PF	25.00
1995 25 Rupees, arms/da Gama (S), PF	37.50

Seychelles 1974 5 Rupees

SOLOMON ISLANDS	BU
1977 2 Cents, Elizabeth II/eagle spirit (C)	.50
1988 10 Cents, Elizabeth II/sea spirit (CN)	1.00
1996 50 Cents, Elizabeth II/arms (CN, 12-sided)	3.00
1992 10 Dollars, Elizabeth II/crocodile (S), PF	35.00
2000 25 Dollars, Elizabeth II/sailing ship (S), PF	245.00

Solomon Islands 1992 10 Dollars

Solomon Islands 2000 25 Dollars

UNION OF SOUTH AFRICA	VF
1931 1/4 Penny, George V/two sparrows (C)	1.50
1942 1/4 Penny, George VI/two sparrows (C)	.50
1929 1/2 Penny, George V/ship (C)	5.00
1953 1/2 Penny, Elizabeth II/ship (C)	.35
1952 Penny, George VI/ship (C)	.50
1953 Penny, Elizabeth II/ship (C)	.35
1927 3 Pence, George V/Protea plant within three stick bundles (S)	2.50
1943 3 Pence, George VI/similar (S)	1.00
1924 6 Pence, George V/wreath (S)	12.50
1927 6 Pence, George V/Protea plant within six stick bundles (S)	4.00
1957 6 Pence, Elizabeth II/similar (S)	.75
1943 Shilling, George VI/allegory of Cape of Good Hope (S)	2.00
1953 Shilling, Elizabeth II/similar (S)	1.50
1932 2 Shillings, George V/shield (S)	6.00
1942 2 Shillings, George VI/shield (S)	4.00
1932 2-1/2 Shillings, George V/crowned shield (S)	8.00
1955 2-1/2 Shillings, Elizabeth II/similar (S)	3.75
1952 5 Shillings, George VI/ship (S)	7.50
1953 5 Shillings, Elizabeth II/springbok (S)	7.50
1958 5 Shillings, similar	7.00
1923 Sovereign, George V/horseman (G)	300.00
1945 Rupee, George VI/wreath (S)	3.50
1947 Rupee, George VI/tiger (N)	2.50

Union of South Africa 1953 5 Shillings

Union of South Africa 1923 Sovereign

SOUTHERN RHODESIA	VF
1936 Penny, crowned rose (CN)	1.25
1942 6 Pence, George VI/two hatchets (S)	7.50
1947 Shilling, George VI/stone bird (CN)	1.50
1932 2 Shillings, George V/antelope (S)	12.00
1951 2 Shillings, George VI/antelope (CN)	3.00
1954 2 Shillings, Elizabeth II/antelope (CN)	35.00
1932 Half Crown, George V/crowned shield (S)	10.00
1953 Crown, Elizabeth II/Cecil Rhodes (S)	12.50

Southern Rhodesia 1932 2 Shillings

STRAITS SETTLEMENTS	VF
1916 1/4 Cent, George V (C)	15.00
1908 1 Cent, Edward VII (C)	10.00
1926 1 Cent, George V (C, square)	1.50
1901 5 Cents, Victoria (S)	15.00
1927 10 Cents, George V (S)	2.00
1910 20 Cents, Edward VII (S)	12.00
1920 50 Cents, George V (S)	7.50
1920 Dollar, George V/ornamental design containing Chinese and Malay inscription (S)	50.00

Straits Settlements 1908 Cent

Straits Settlements 1920 Dollar

CAUCASUS

The first modern, European-style coins produced in this region were copper and silver issues struck by Georgia (1804-1833) while under czarist Russian influence. It was not until the breakup of the Soviet Union that local coinage of the Caucasus region was again produced. The first coins were aluminum Azerbaijani and Armenian coins. Both were of fairly plain design. Well-made coins with attractive reverse designs were introduced by Georgia in 1993. A limited number of collector issues have been struck by Georgia and Armenia.

Known Counterfeits: none.

ARMENIA	BU
1994 10 Luma, arms (AL)	.50
1994 3 Drams, arms (AL)	1.25
1996 100 Drams, Bagramian/arms (S), PF	300.00
1996 100 Drams, stork with chess board/arms (CN)	9.00
1997 25,000 Drams, Anahit (G), PF	200.00

AZERBAIJAN	BU
1992 10 Qapik, eight-pointed star (AL)	2.50
1993 20 Qapik, crescent and star (AL)	1.00
1996 50 Manat, Mohammed Fuzuli (S)	50.00
1999 50 Manat, horseman, PF	70.00

Armenia 1996 100 Drams

GEORGIA	BU
1993 20 Thetri, emblem/stag (St.)	2.00
1995 500 Lari, profiles of Stalin, Roosevelt, Churchill and de Gaulle (G), PF	520.00
2000 10 Lari, eagle, lion (S), PF	55.00

Georgia 2000 10 Lari

CZECHOSLOVAKIA

After 400 years of Austrian rule, Czechoslovakia became an independent state in 1918, following the breakup of the Hapsburg Empire. Although most of the coins circulating here were regular issues of the empire, special copper pieces were struck for Bohemia in the late 1700s. Also common were coins struck by the local bishops of Olmuetz.

Known Counterfeits: few.

BOHEMIA & MORAVIA	VF
1943 1 Koruna, double-tailed lion/ivy branches (Z)	.75

CZECHOSLOVAKIA	VF
1925 10 Haleru, double-tailed lion/bridge (C)	.35
1938 20 Haleru, double-tailed lion/wheat and scythe (CN)	.35
1922 1 Koruna, double-tailed lion/woman with sheaf and scythe (CN)	.50
1934 20 Korun, shield/three figures standing (S)	6.50

	BU
1949 50 Korun, Stalin/shield (S)	8.00
1965 10 Korun, shield/Jan Hus (S)	20.00
1966 5 Haleru, shield/wreath (AL)	.50
1980 2 Koruny, shield/symbol (CN)	1.00
1991 5 Haleru, CSFR over shield/5h (AL)	.50
1981 100 Korun, spaniel/arms (S)	10.00
1993 500 Korun, shield/tennis player (S)	40.00

Czechoslovakia 1922 Koruna

Czechoslovakia 1965 10 Korun

Czechoslovakia 1992 500 Korun

CZECH REPUBLIC	BU
1993 1 Koruna, double-tailed lion/crown (N-clad St.)	1.00
1993 50 Korun, double-tailed lion/city view (B, St., C)	9.00
1994 200 Korun, shield/cathedral (S)	14.50

Czech Republic 1994 200 Korun

SLOVAKIA	VF
1939 10 Halierov, shield/castle (C)	2.00
1941 1 Koruna, shield/wreath (CN)	1.00
1944 10 Korun, shield/king, bishop and knight (S)	4.00
	BU
1993 10 Halierov, shield/steeple (AL)	.50
1993 10 Koruna, shield/medieval cross (B)	3.00
1993 100 Korun, shield/three doves (S)	10.00
1994 200 Korun, logo/hockey player (S)	18.00

Slovakia 1944 10 Korun

FRANCE

After centuries of deterioration, French royal coinage stabilized somewhat by the 1600s. This coincides with the introduction of milled coinage of neat manufacture. A silver-dollar-sized ecu and its fractions became common. Small values were struck in base silver and especially copper. This included the old denier tournois, which had survived since the 1200s. The gold louis d'or became so recognized for its stability that it saw wide circulation internationally. Most coins bore the king's portrait, with fleurs or a shield of arms on the reverse. Sometimes an elaborate cross or monogram, held over from the Renaissance, was still used. Despite the improved striking methods, imprecise means were used to manufacture blanks of exact weight; so many had to be adjusted with a file before striking to remove excess metal. The resulting "adjustment marks" are not damage, but if they are severe, they do reduce the coin's value.

Among the most important aspects of French coinage history is the effect the French Revolution had on iconography. A new set of symbols replaced the traditional ones. Those reflecting new ideologies include one displaying a tablet inscribed: "Men are equal before the law." An allegorical head, initially representing liberty, was also quite popular. Even after Napoleon took the reins as emperor, he temporarily maintained the revolutionary name of the country as "French Republic" on the coinage. The revolution's most lasting change on the coinage was the decimal system. This system, used the world over today, divides the monetary unit, the franc or the dollar, for example, into tenths or hundredths.

Most 19th-century French coin designs were conservative, depicting the monarch and a coat of arms or value. There was, however, great artistic merit in the beautiful coins of 1898 to 1920.

In this dawn of the new European currency, the euro, it is all the more important to mention that French coinage was the basis of an earlier international currency, that of the Latin Monetary Union, from 1865 to 1920. During this period, the money of nations as diverse as Greece and Switzerland were struck on an international standard and held the same value.

The most common design used by the French republics was an allegorical female head or bust. This image, tracing its roots to a 1790s allegory of liberty, is variously described today as the personification of the republic of France, and as Marie Anne (the personification's nickname).

Inflation hit France after World War I, and the currency did not stabilize until 1960. During this time, most of the coins were of baser metals, including aluminum-bronze and aluminum. Some denominations were distinguished with holes in their centers. Many mintmarks were used on French coins before 1960, and some of the dates and mintmarks can be valuable. Only common ones for the type are listed here. Coins before 1960, and some outmoded ones struck afterward, have no legal-tender status.

In January 2002, France replaced the franc with coins denominated in euros, the currency of the European Union. Some coins were struck as early as 1999 and held until 2002. On the circulating denominations, 1 cent through 2 euros, one side carries a French design, the other a common European design. On higher-denomination commemoratives, both sides are distinctively French.

Colonial coins from India are the earliest common French colonials. Many of these are hardly distinguishable from local Indian States coins. Usually they are identified by certain symbols, such as a fleur or a cock. They were originally intended to circulate alongside crude local coins, and their designs and crudeness made this possible.

Other colonial coins were struck occasionally from the 1890s through the 1930s but were not abundant except in Indo-China. During World War I, and especially right after, however, they were struck in abundant quantities in base metals. Usually one side bore a female head representing an allegory of France. The reverse alluded to the individual colony. Since 1948, virtually all French colonial coins can be easily collected in mint state.

Known Counterfeits: Contemporary counterfeits of French coins have always been common. The gold 20- and 50-franc pieces should be examined with care. Counterfeits of smaller denominations are slightly less dangerous. A sampling of counterfeit French coins includes the 1915 franc and 1960 and 1975 5-franc, but hundreds of others exist.

RESTORED REPUBLIC, 1871-1958	VF
1908 2 Centimes, Republic head (C)	.75
1916 5 Centimes, similar/allegorical group (C)	.75
1916 10 Centimes, head r./allegorical scene (C)	.75
1922 10 Centimes, cap, RF (CN, holed)	.75
1931 10 Centimes, cap, RF (CN, holed)	.35
1945 20 Centimes, similar (Z)	4.00
1904 25 Centimes, Republic head/fasces (N)	.75
1916 50 Centimes, sower (S)	1.00
1939 50 Centimes, head l. (ALB)	.25
1946 50 Centimes, head l. (AL)	.25
1943 1 Franc, axe (AL)	.25
1947 1 Franc, head l./cornucopia (AL)	.15
1915 2 Francs, sower (S)	3.50
1921 2 Francs, Mercury seated (ALB)	1.50
1945 5 Francs, head l./wreath (AL)	.35
1901 10 Francs, head l./cock l. (G)	85.00
1952 10 Francs, head l./cock and branch (ALB)	.35
1933 20 Francs, head l./two ears of grain (S)	6.00
1953 50 Francs, head l./cock and branch (ALB)	1.00
1909 100 Francs, winged genius (G)	865.00
1955 100 Francs, bust with torch/branches (CN)	.75

France 1922 10 Centimes

France 1904 25 Centimes

France 1946 50 Centimes

France 1943 Franc

France 1964 5 Francs

France 1952 10 Francs

VICHY FRANCE	VF
1941 20 Centimes, VINGT over oak leaves (Z, holed)	2.00
1941 20 Centimes, 20 over oak leaves (Z, holed)	2.00
1943 1 Franc, ax between wheatears (AL)	.25
1941 5 Francs, Philippe Petain/ax (CN)	100.00

FIFTH REPUBLIC, 1959-DATE	BU
1968 1 Centime, wheatear (St.)	.35
1987 5 Centimes, bust l. (ALB)	.15
1967 20 Centimes, bust l. (ALB)	.25
1976 1/2 Franc, sower (N)	.50
1970 1 Franc, sower (N)	.60
1979 2 Francs, modernistic sower (N)	1.00
1974 10 Francs, map/girders (NB)	2.50
1989 10 Francs, winged genius (St. in ALB)	7.50
1989 10 Francs, montesquieu (St. in ALB)	20.00
1986 100 Francs, Statue of Liberty (S)	16.50
1987 100 Francs, LaFayette (S)	25.00
1996 100 Francs, clovis (S)	37.50
1990 500 Francs = 70 Ecus, Charlemagne (G), PF	500.00

EURO COINAGE	BU
1999 20 Euro Cent, sower/map (B, notched edge)	1.50

France 1986 100 Francs

FRENCH COLONIAL

ALGERIA	VF
1956 20 Francs, head r./two wheatears (CN)	2.50
1949 50 Francs, similar (CN)	3.00
1952 100 Francs, similar (CN)	4.00

CAMEROON	VF
1943 50 Centimes, cock/double cross (C)	3.50
1926 1 Franc, head l./palm branches (ALB)	2.00
1948 1 Franc, antelope head (AL)	.35
1924 2 Francs, head l./palm branches (ALB)	15.00

Cameroon 1948 Franc

COMOROS	BU
1964 1 Franc, head l./palm trees (AL)	4.00
1964 5 Francs, similar (AL)	6.00
1964 10 Francs, shells and Coelacanth fish (ALB)	4.00

Comoros 1964 5 Francs

FRENCH AFARS & ISSAS	BU
1975 2 Francs, antelope head (AL)	6.00
1968 5 Francs, similar (AL)	7.00
1975 20 Francs, ocean liner and small sailing ship (ALB)	8.00
1975 50 Francs, head l./two camels (CN)	12.00

French Afars & Issas 1968 5 Francs

FRENCH EQUATORIAL AFRICA	XF
1943 5 Centimes, cap over RF (ALB, holed)	325.00
1943 50 Centimes, cock/double cross (C)	7.00
1942 1 Franc, similar (B)	10.00
1948 1 Franc, head l./antelope head (AL)	.50
1948 2 Francs, similar (AL)	1.50

French Equatorial Africa 1948 Franc

FRENCH INDO-CHINA	VF
1921 10 Cents, Liberty/denomination (S)	3.00
1903 Piastre, Liberty/denomination in wreath (S)	18.00
	XF
1942 1/4 Cent, (Z)	35.00
1935 1/2 Cent, cap over RF (C)	2.00
1943 1 Cent, ears of grain (AL)	4.00
1939 5 Cents, head above two cornucopias (NB, holed)	5.00
1946 5 Cents, bust with olive branch (AL)	1.00
1941 10 Cents, similar (CN)	3.00
1941 20 Cents, similar (CN)	2.00
1936 50 Cents, figure seated (S)	12.00
1931 Piastre, head l. (S)	40.00
1947 Piastre, bust with olive branch (CN)	7.50

French Indo-China 1903 Piastre

French Indo-China 1941 20 Cents

FRENCH OCEANIA	XF
1949 50 Centimes, Republic seated/beach scene (AL)	1.50
1949 2 Francs, similar (AL)	1.25

French Oceania 1949 2 Francs

FRENCH POLYNESIA	BU
1965 50 Centimes, Republic seated/beach scene (AL)	4.50
1987 1 Franc, similar (AL)	1.25
1965 2 Francs, similar (AL)	2.50
1967 10 Francs, carving (N)	4.75
1991 50 Francs, beach huts below mountain (N)	5.00
1982 100 Francs, similar (N-C)	8.50

French Polynesia 1982 100 Francs

FRENCH SOMALILAND	BU
1959 1 Franc (AL)	5.00
1965 1 Franc, antelope head (AL)	6.00
1959 2 Francs, similar (AL)	7.00
1965 10 Francs, ocean liner and small sailing ship (ALB)	8.00

French Somaliland 1959 Franc

FRENCH WEST AFRICA	XF
1944 1 Franc, head l./two cornucopias (ALB)	10.00
1948 2 Francs, head l./antelope head (AL)	.50
1956 10 Francs, similar (ALB)	1.50
1957 25 Francs, antelope head/root figure (ALB)	2.00

French West Africa 1948 2 Francs

GUADELOUPE	F
1921 50 Centimes, Carib Indian (CN)	12.00
1903 1 Franc, Carib Indian (CN)	20.00
MADAGASCAR	XF
1943 50 Centimes, cock/double cross (C)	10.00
1958 1 Franc, three bull heads (AL)	.75
1948 2 Francs, similar (AL)	.85
1953 20 Francs, map (ALB)	3.00

Madagascar 1958 Franc

MARTINIQUE	F

1922 50 Centimes, bust of contemporary woman (CN)   25.00

Martinique 1922 Franc

NEW CALEDONIA	BU
1949 50 Centimes, Republic seated/Kagu bird (AL)	7.50
1994 1 Franc, similar (AL)	1.25
1949 2 Francs, similar (AL)	5.50
1972 10 Francs, small sailing ship (N)	5.25
1967 20 Francs, busts of three bulls	8.50
1972 50 Francs, hut and trees (N)	7.00
1976 100 Francs, similar (N-C)	9.00

New Caledonia 1949 50 Centimes

New Caledonia 1972 50 Francs

NEW HEBRIDES	BU
1970 1 Franc, bird (NB)	1.75
1973 10 Francs, carved head (N)	2.75
1966 100 Francs, carving (S)	25.00

New Hebrides 1973 10 Francs

New Hebrides 1966 100 Francs

REUNION	BU
1948 1 Franc, sugar cane plants (AL)	3.00
1955 10 Francs, shield (ALB)	3.50
1964 100 Francs, shield (N)	5.00

Reunion 1948 Franc

SAINT PIERRE & MIQUELON	BU
1948 1 Franc, sailing ship (AL)	15.00
1948 2 Francs, similar (AL)	15.00

Saint Pierre & Miquelon 1948 Franc

TOGO	VF
1924 50 Centimes, palm branches (ALB)	20.00
1948 1 Franc, antelope head (AL)	12.00
1924 2 Francs, head/palm branches (ALB)	35.00
1925 2 Francs, palm branches (ALB)	38.00
1956 5 Francs, antelope head (ALB)	6.00

Togo 1924 2 Francs

TONKIN   **XF**

1905 1/600th Piastre, French inscription/Chinese inscription (Z)   20.00

Tonkin 1905 1/600th Piastre

TUNISIA	VF
1938 5 Centimes, Arabic inscription/French inscription (CN, holed)	4.00
1945 50 Centimes, wreath/wreath (ALB)	1.00
1946 5 Francs, Arabic inscription/French inscription (ALB)	1.50
1939 20 Francs, two branches/wreath (S)	20.00

Tunisia 1939 20 Francs

GERMANY

The coinage of Germany is by far the most complex of the modern era. As more and more nobles and bishops were given the right to strike coins as a favor of the Holy Roman emperor, the number of issuing authorities in greater Germany became almost bewildering. At its greatest, it ran into several hundred. Most coins were solely in their own names; others, such as cities, cited their own authority on one side but paid homage to the Holy Roman emperor on the other. The local side of a coin would usually depict the bust or arms of the local prince or a city's patron saint. Some depicted symbolic animals or a wildman (a giant wearing nothing but a loin-encircling bush).

The emperor was sometimes portrayed, but usually he was honored by inscribing his titles around a double-headed eagle. Usually, the emperor was the head of the Austrian house of Hapsburg, but not always.

Following the Napoleonic wars, many of the ecclesiastical territories were absorbed by the secular ones, the greater states began to take over the smaller ones, and the Holy Roman Empire ceased to exist. For the first time, the number of coin-issuing German states began to decline. This process continued until the German states were finally replaced by a republic in 1918.

There were a great many local coinage standards, but some basic ideas remained consistent. A thaler was a large, silver-dollar-sized coin. A ducat was made of gold and uniformly contained

11/100 troy ounces of that metal. Good silver coins were often valued in terms of how many made a thaler. Thus, the inscription "6 einen thaler" meant the coin was worth one-sixth of a thaler. Guldens were not always used, but when they were, they usually resembled an American half dollar. The albus and groschen were small silver coins. Other small coins—such as the pfennig, heller, or kreuzer—could be copper or billon, but they were originally silver when created in the Middle Ages.

Almost 50 years before the German States passed into history, Germany became a unified nation. Each local prince retained his own territories and some aspect of local government, but after 1871, the national government fell to the hands of one German emperor, who happened to be the hereditary king of Prussia, the most powerful of the German states. Throughout Germany, all copper and small silver coins (1 pfennig to 1 mark) were uniform. Larger silver and gold coins (2 through 20 marks) shared a common reverse design with the legend Deutsches Reich. The obverse bore the portrait of the local prince or the city arms.

During and immediately after World War I, hundreds of municipal governments and companies throughout Germany struck small-denomination emergency tokens, or notgeld, to facilitate commerce. They were usually struck in zinc, iron or aluminum, occasionally porcelain. Their designs run from traditionally heraldic to humorous to utilitarian.

The Weimar Republic of 1918 to 1933 struck minor coins of fairly bland agricultural designs and a good number of exciting commemorative silver pieces. Its coins were replaced in the 1930s by ones bearing the notorious Nazi swastika held by an eagle. During World War II, as in so many other countries, zinc replaced most coinage metals needed for the war effort.

From 1949 until 1990, there were two Germanies: the Federal Republic (West) and the smaller, Soviet-dominated Democratic Republic (East). Each had its own coinage, the West with a traditional German eagle, the East with typical Communist industrial symbolism. Both states struck numerous commemoratives, often similar in inspiration. With the fall of communism, East Germany chose to join West Germany, which then attempted to bail the smaller state out of the economic morass of communism.

In January 2002, Germany replaced the mark with coins denominated in euros, the currency of the European Union. On the circulating denominations, 1 cent through 2 euros, one side carries a German design, the other a common European design. On higher-denomination commemoratives, both sides are distinctively German.

The German Empire struck coins for two colonies, and both are popularly collected. The issues for German East Africa were struck in gold, silver and bronze. These large silver pieces bear an exciting bust of Kaiser Wilhelm II wearing an elaborate griffin-topped helmet. The large silver pieces of German New Guinea display a detailed bird of paradise, considered by some to be among the most beautiful images of the entire European colonial series. All German New Guinea coins are scarce and in high demand.

German States, Mecklenburg-Schwerin 1904 2 Mark

GERMAN STATES (All reverses are the imperial eagle unless noted.)	VF
Anhalt-Dessau, 1914 3 Mark, heads of duke and duchess (S)	60.00
Baden, 1908 3 Mark, head of Friedrich II l. (S)	25.00
Bavaria, 1909 3 Mark, head of Otto l. (S)	18.00
Bremen, 1904 2 Mark, shield (S)	70.00
Brunswick-Wolfenbuttel, 1915 3 Mark, heads of duke and duchess r. (S)	120.00
Hesse-Darmstadt, 1904 2 Mark, busts of Philipp and Ludwig l. (S)	65.00
Lippe-Detmold, 1906 2 Mark, bust of Leopold IV l. (S)	225.00
Lübeck, 1908 3 Mark, double-headed eagle (S)	70.00
Mecklenburg-Schwerin, 1904 2 Mark, busts of grand duke and grand duchess l. (S)	40.00
Oldenburg, 1901 2 Mark, bust of Friedrich August l. (S)	225.00
Prussia, 1913 2 Mark, bust of Wilhelm II (S)	15.00
1913 3 Mark, King on horse, surrounded by followers/eagle grasping snake (S)	20.00

GERMAN STATES (All reverses are the imperial eagle unless noted.)	VF
1908 5 Mark, Wilhelm II (S)	16.00
Saxe-Altenburg, 1903 5 Mark, bust of Ernst r. (S)	200.00
Saxe-Coburg-Gotha, 1905 2 Mark, head of Carl Eduard r. (S)	350.00
Saxe-Meiningen, 1915 2 Mark, bust of Georg II l. (S)	75.00
Saxe-Weimar-Eisenach, 1910 3 Mark, heads of grand duke and grand duchess (S)	40.00
Saxony, 1913 3 Mark, building (S)	18.00
Schaumburg-Lippe, 1911 3 Mark, bust of Georg l. (S)	65.00
Schwarzburg-Sondershausen, 1905 2 Mark, head of Karl Günther r. (S)	90.00
Waldeck-Pyrmont, 1903 20 Mark, head of Friedrich l. (G)	4,500.00
Württemberg, 1914 3 Mark, bust of Wilhelm II r. (S)	17.50
1904 10 Mark, similar (G)	140.00

German States, Schaumburg-Lippe 1911 3 Mark

GERMAN EMPIRE 1873-1918	VF
1915 1 Pfennig, large eagle/inscription (C)	1.00
1906 2 Pfennig, similar (C)	1.00
1905 5 Pfennig, large eagle (CN)	.75
1919 5 Pfennig, similar (iron)	.50
1902 10 Pfennig, similar (CN)	1.00
1905 10 Pfennig, similar (CN)	.50
1909 25 Pfennig, large eagle/wreath (N)	9.00
1918 1/2 Mark, eagle in wreath/wreath (S)	1.50
1914 1 Mark, large eagle/wreath (S)	2.25

German Empire 1902 10 Pfennig

NOTGELD	VF
Aachen, 1920 10 Pfennig, bear (iron)	3.00
Coblenz, 1918 25 Pfennig, arms (iron)	2.50
Darmstadt, 1917 10 Pfennig, crowned arms (Z)	2.00
Hamburg, 1923 5/100 Verrechnungsmarke, arms (AL)	4.00
Leipzig, (1920) 20 Pfennig, arms/Strassenbahn (iron)	3.00
similar but wooded	5.00
Westphalia, 1923 1/4 Million Mark, Von Stein/horse rearing (AL)	6.00

WEIMAR REPUBLIC 1919-1933	VF
1923 1 Rentenpfennig, sheaf of wheat (C)	1.00
1925 2 Reichspfennig, similar (C)	.50
1932 4 Reichspfenning, eagle (C)	12.00
1924 5 Reichspfennig, stylized wheat (ALB)	.60
1925 5 Reichspfennig, similar (ALB)	.50
1929 10 Reichspfennig, similar (ALB)	1.00
1924 50 Rentenpfennig, similar (ALB)	12.00
1931 50 Reichspfennig, eagle (N)	4.00
1924 1 Mark, eagle (S)	12.00
1922 3 Mark, eagle within legend (AL)	2.50
1928 3 Reichsmark, eagle/Dinkelsbühl, man over city walls (S)	500.00
1930 5 Reichsmark, eagle/Graf zeppelin (S)	120.00
1931 5 Reichsmark, eagle/oak tree (S)	100.00

German Republic 1932 4 Reichspfennig

NAZI STATE 1933-1945	VF
1937 1 Reichspfennig, eagle holding swastika in wreath (C)	.35
1940 5 Reichspfennig, similar (Z)	.25
1938 50 Reichspfennig, similar (N)	30.00
1941 50 Reichspfennig, similar (AL)	10.00
1934 2 Reichsmark, Schiller (S)	70.00
1936 5 Reichsmark, Hindenburg/eagle holding swastika in wreath (S)	6.00

Nazi State 1936 5 Reichsmark

FEDERAL REPUBLIC	Unc.
1950 1 Pfennig, oak sapling (C-plated St.)	2.00
1993 2 Pfennig, oak sapling (C-plated St.)	4.00
1949 5 Pfennig, oak sapling (B-plated St.)	40.00
1980 10 Pfennig, oak sapling (B-plated St.)	.20
1950 50 Pfennig, woman planting sapling (CN)	7.00
1977 1 Deutsche Mark, eagle/oak leaves (CN)	3.00
1951 2 Deutsche Mark, eagle/grapes and wheat (CN)	100.00
1971 2 Deutsche Mark, Max Planck/eagle (CN)	3.00
1952 5 Deutsche Mark, museum, stylized eagle/eagle (S)	800.00
1968 5 Deutsche Mark, bust of Gutenberg/eagle (S)	9.00
1970 5 Deutsche Mark, eagle/inscription (S)	10.00
1976 5 Deutsche Mark, monster/eagle (S)	6.00
1983 5 Deutsche Mark, Karl Marx/eagle (CN-clad N)	4.00
1972 10 Deutsche Mark, Olympic flame/eagle (S)	7.00
1990 10 Deutsche Mark, Friedrich Barbarossa/eagle (S)	7.00

German Federal Republic 1950 Pfennig

German Federal Republic 1980 10 Pfennig

German Federal Republic 1968 5 Deutsche Mark

DEMOCRATIC REPUBLIC (EAST GERMANY)	Unc.
1952 1 Pfennig, hammer, compass and wheat (AL)	7.00
1948 5 Pfennig, wheat on gear (AL)	65.00
1989 10 Pfennig, hammer and compass within wheat (AL)	2.00
1950 50 Pfennig, three smoke stacks (ALB)	150.00
1982 2 Mark, hammer and compass within wheat (AL)	3.00
1971 5 Mark, Brandenburg Gate (CN)	10.00
1979 5 Mark, Albert Einstein (CN)	75.00
1972 10 Mark, Buchenwald Memorial (CN)	8.00
1988 10 Mark, knight/arms (S)	90.00
1988 20 Mark, microscope (S)	250.00

German Democratic Republic 1988 10 Mark

GERMAN EAST AFRICA	VF
1910 Heller, crown/wreath (C)	1.50
1909 5 Heller, similar (C)	50.00
1916 5 Heller, crown over DOA/wreath (B)	20.00
1913 1/4 Rupie, bust of Wilhelm II in griffin helmet/wreath (S)	12.00
1916 15 Rupien, eagle/elephant (G)	1,000.00

German East Africa 1909 5 Heller

German East Africa 1916 15 Rupien

HUNGARY

The reign of Leopold I the Hogmouth (1657-1705) saw a far greater change for Hungarian coins than it did for the coinage of his Austrian dominions. Of course, as in Austria, modern coin production under Leopold, using roller dies, was taken to a new height of uniformity. Their excellent portraits are perfect examples of the baroque style. Collectors should be aware that coins struck with roller dies usually appear slightly curved; this is not a flaw. But in Hungary before the mid-1600s, only three denominations—the small base-silver denar, the big silver thaler, and the gold ducat—were common in circulation. This period saw increased production of a whole range of middle denominations. For the most part, the Madonna-and-child design still dominated the reverse, with portraits on the obverse.

During Maria Theresa's reign (1740-80), copper replaced base silver for the small denominations, and coats of arms became more common. The coppers in particular were ornamented with impressive, high-relief portraits. Unfortunately, the poor condition of most surviving examples makes this difficult to appreciate today.

From 1892 until the communist takeover, the holy crown of Saint Stephen, a relic of Hungary's patron saint, dominated the coinage, with the Madonna or a portrait for diversity. The communists replaced the old religious symbols with national heroes, architecture, and images idealizing industrial and agricultural labor. Interestingly, the new post-communist republic combines old and new imagery harmoniously, with a pleasant added mixture of flora and fauna.

Known Counterfeits: Many gold coins have been restruck in quantity. These include 1907 and 1908 100 korona. Also note that all coins marked "UP" are restrikes, regardless of type or metal.

Francis Joseph, 1848-1916	VF
1909 2 Filler, crown of St. Stephen (C)	1.00
1915 Korona, head r./crown of St. Stephen (S)	3.00
1908 5 Korona, similar (S)	18.00
1901 20 Korona Francis Joseph, standing/arms (G)	180.00
Regency, 1920-1945	**VF**
1937 2 Filler, crown of St. Stephen (C)	.25
1938 2 Filler, crown of St. Stephen (C)	.20
1927 1 Pengo, crowned shield (S)	1.75
1942 2 Pengo, similar (AL)	.30
1938 5 Pengo, bust of St. Stephen/arms (S)	10.00
1943 5 Pengo, bust of Nicholas Horthy/arms (AL)	1.00

Hungary 1937 2 Filler

Republics, 1946-date	BU
1950 2 Filler, wreath (AL, holed)	.75
1982 10 Filler, dove (AL)	1.75
1979 50 Filler, bridge (AL)	1.75
1979 200 Forint, IYC logo (S)	12.00
1949 1 Forint, arms (AL)	20.00
1971 5 Forint, Kossuth/arms (N)	1.75
1956 25 Forint, parliament/arms and gear (S)	25.00
1985 100 Forint, turtle (CNZ)	14.00
1961 500 Forint, Bela Bartok (G), PF	1,200.00
1997 5 Forint, egret (B)	1.50
1996 100 Forint, crowned shield (St., B-plated center)	4.50
2000 200 Forint, Rhodin's Thinker and solar system/arms (B)	6.00
1992 500 Forint, Tellstar satellite (S)	25.00
same but proof	27.50

Hungary 1985 100 Forint

Hungary 2000 200 Forint

ITALY

Much like Germany, Italy was divided into a number of smaller independent countries until 1861. During most of the modern era, the south was unified as one kingdom, the Kingdom of Naples and Sicily (more properly called the Two Sicilies). Although artistically creative in the 1600s and 1700s, its more mundane later coinage is more commonly encountered. The island of Sicily usually had separate coinage.

Central Italy was ruled by the pope. Despite being one unified papal state, many of the larger cities under papal rule had special designs and sometimes even different coinage standards. This local variation ended by 1800. Unlike the other Italian states incorporated into the new unified Kingdom of Italy in 1860-61, the pope was able to maintain his independence until 1870. After decades of dispute with Italy, the papal state restored its independence in 1929 as the much smaller State of the Vatican City. Since then, papal coins have been routinely struck and can occasionally be found circulating not only at the Vatican but also in and around Rome. Most Vatican coins today are collected in mint sets.

Throughout this period, most papal and Vatican coins have depicted the pope or his coat of arms, along with some religious iconography or a Latin saying reflecting some moral precept. There are three kinds of "special" coins. Sede Vacante coins are struck between popes and have the arms of the papal secretary of state. Holy Year coins are struck to celebrate the Jubilee, when pilgrims are encouraged to come to Rome. Last, Lateran coins were given to the crowds when the pope took possession of the Cathedral of St. John Lateran in Rome. This is his church as bishop of Rome, not St. Peter's Basilica.

Papal medals are quite common and are struck for commemorative purposes only. They should not be confused with coins. They are usually large and have very high relief. Most of those dated before 1775 are actually government restrikes, struck from the original dies from the late 1700s and later. Those after 1550 that appear cast are unofficial replicas but not necessarily worthless.

Northern Italy was much more complex. It was a variable mix of small states. Some, such as Venice, were international powers; others were controlled by petty princes. Ultimately a good number of them fell into the hands of foreign powers, such as Spain, France and Austria. The duke of Savoy (who was also king of Sardinia) began to unify Italy by conquering these small states and then moving south. One Italian state that has survived is San Marino. It has had coinage since 1864, but today most of its coins are sold to collectors. Like the Vatican's coins, they are struck to Italian standards and can be spent in Italy.

The first unified Italian coinage was struck to the standard of the international Latin Monetary Union (see France). Italian coins of the 20th century are usually of high artistic merit. After World War I, the lira shrunk to one fifth of its previous value. Its value decreased again after World War II, and many coins minted from the 1940s to the 1980s were made from aluminum or steel.

In January 2002, Italy replaced the lira with coins denominated in euros, the currency of the European Union. On the circulating denominations, 1 cent through 2 euros, one side carries an Italian design, the other a common European design. Because of their monetary unions with Italy, the Vatican and San Marino have euro coins struck out of Italy's allotment of coinage.

The colonial coins of Italy are popularly collected and in high demand. Most silver is found cleaned and most copper pitted, but despite this, collectors often settle for these imperfect specimens.

Known Counterfeits: There are many contemporary counterfeits of Italian minors, including the 1911 2 lire; 1927 and 1930 5 lire; and 1958 500 lire. More dangerous counterfeits capable of fooling collectors are quite common. Most are imitations of the old silver-dollar-size 5 and 20 lire. This is also true of similar papal and San Marino 5 lire. The overwhelming majority of Eritrea 5 lire and Talero pieces are counterfeit. Many Italian, papal, and Vatican gold coins have also been counterfeited but less commonly than the large silver. A list includes the 1914 5 lire. Authentic common coins are sometimes found altered to rare dates. The 20 lire depicting Mussolini is not a coin but a privately struck fantasy.

VITTORIO EMANUELE III, 1900-1946	VF
1915 2 Centesimi, bust l./Italia on ship (C)	3.00
1921 10 Centesimi, head l./bee (C)	.75
1908 20 Centesimi, head l./lady (N)	2.00
1940 20 Centesimi, head l./allegorical head r. with fasces (St.)	.40
1922 1 Lira, Italia seated (N)	2.00
1924 2 Lire, bust r./fasces (N)	5.00
1914 5 Lire, bust r./Italia in four-horse chariot (S)	8,000.00
1927 5 Lire, head l./eagle (S)	5.00
1927 10 Lire, head l./Italia in two-horse chariot (S)	30.00
1927 20 Lire, head r./naked youth before seated Italia (S)	250.00
1943 20 Lire, Mussolini/fasces and lion head (Silvered B), (This is a common postwar fantasy.)	6.00 BU
1912 50 Lire, bust l./Italia and plow (G)	1,600.00

Italy 1908 20 Centesimi

Italy 1927 5 Lire

Italy 1927 20 Lire

Republic, 1946-date	BU
1954 1 Lira, scales/cornucopia (AL)	2.50
1957 2 Lire, bee (AL)	6.00
1969 5 Lire, rudder/porpoise (AL)	1.00
1950 10 Lire, Pegasus (AL)	35.00
1975 50 Lire, Vulcan at forge (St.)	1.00
1956 100 Lire, Minerva presenting olive tree (St.)	60.00
1974 100 Lire, Minerva presenting olive tree (St.)	1.00
1974 100 Lire, Marconi (St.)	2.00
1959 500 Lire, Renaissance bust/Columbus' ships (S)	12.00
1986 500 Lire, Donatello/Donatello's David (S)	45.00
1970 1,000 Lire, Concordia/Campidoglio pattern (S)	20.00

Italy 1956 100 Lire

ERITREA	VF
1918 Tallero, female bust r./eagle (S)	100.00

ITALIAN SOMALILAND	VF
1909 1 Besa, bust l. (C)	30.00
1919 1/2 Rupia, head r./crown and wreath (S)	60.00
1925 5 Lire, bust r./arms (S)	300.00

Most of the tallero-size coins of Eritrea and Italian Somaliland on the market are counterfeit.

SAN MARINO	XF
1935 5 Centesimi, arms (C)	12.00
1906 1 Lira, arms/wreath (S)	40.00

	BU
1972 1 Lira, bust of St. Marino (AL)	.50
1974 20 Lire, three towers/lobster (ALB)	2.50
1974 Scudo, arms/saint standing (G)	90.00
1992 100 Lire, similar/Columbus' ships (St.)	1.50
1982 500 Lire, similar/Garibaldi (S)	15.00
1996 10,000 Lire, arms/wolves (S), PF	60.00
1979 5 Scudi, three palm fronds/three arms (G)	445.00

San Marino 1992 100 Lire

Vatican City 1962 5 Lire

VATICAN CITY	BU
1930 5 Centesimi, arms/olive sprig (C)	20.00
1942 10 Centesimi, Pius XII/dove (B)	100.00
1934 20 Centesimi, arms/St. Paul (N)	20.00
1941 50 Centesimi, arms/Archangel Michael (St.)	8.00
1931 1 Lira, arms/Madonna standing (N)	20.00
1942 2 Lire, arms/Justice seated (St.)	5.00
1962 5 Lire, John XXIII/Dove of Holy Spirit (AL)	3.00
1973 10 Lire, arms/fish (AL)	1.50
1985 20 Lire, John Paul II/eagle (ALB)	4.00
1955 50 Lire, Pius XII/Hope (St.)	4.00
1929 100 Lire, Pius XI/Christ standing (G)	800.00
1978 200 Lire, arms/sermon on the mount (ALB)	3.00
1963 500 Lire, Sede Vacante/arms (S)	20.00
1978 1,000 Lire, John Paul I/arms (S)	40.00
1990 1,000 Lire, John Paul II treading over barbed wire/ arms (S)	40.00
2000 2,000 Lire, Pope/baby Jesus (S), PF	75.00
1998 100,000 Lire, John Paul II/Basilica of St. Mary Major (G), PF	600.00

Vatican City 2000 2,000 Lire

LOW COUNTRIES

Belgium, the Netherlands, and Luxembourg are called the "Low Countries" because most of their land is flat and barely above sea level. They are sometimes also called "BeNeLux" after their customs and trade union. All three were controlled by the Spanish Hapsburgs until the late 1500s. At that time, the Netherlands became Protestant and declared its independence. The Spanish Hapsburgs continued to rule Belgium and Luxembourg until 1714, when they were transferred to the Austrian branch of the same dynasty. During the Napoleonic Wars, all three were part of the French empire. After that, a newly independent Kingdom of the Netherlands was given all three territories, only to lose Belgium in 1830 in a revolt resulting from cultural and religious differences. In 1890, Luxembourg was lost when it was decided that the queen of the Netherlands, as a woman, could not legally succeed to the Grand Duchy of Luxembourg.

In addition to royal portraits and heraldry, the coins of Belgium (called Spanish Netherlands and later Austrian Netherlands) and Luxembourg had a few distinctive motifs. These included an X-cross and some purely inscriptional types. A few small territories, such as Liege, had the arms of the local bishop or the bust of a patron saint. The new Kingdom of the Belgians used the international standard of the Latin Monetary Union (see France) until World War I. Interestingly, most Belgian coins are struck in two versions. Some have French and some have Flemish inscriptions, because both languages are commonly spoken.

The coins of the Netherlands have traditionally been struck by its constituent provinces. These almost always had a coat of arms on the copper. Some of the silver coins shared designs from province to province, such as arrows or a knight, but each individual province changed small details, such as the shield and its name in the legend. Thus, they could circulate interchangeably throughout the Netherlands. The lion dalders are particularly common in this series. These are usually poorly struck on irregular blanks. Sea-salvaged examples are worthless, unless accompanied by documentation.

After the new kingdom was founded in 1815, the national arms or the monarch's monogram or portrait were used on a more uniform national coinage. Since the 1500s, Dutch gold ducats with a standing knight have been particularly common in international commerce. The word "BELGII" on their reverses does not refer to Belgium, which did not exist when they were first struck, but to the ancient name for the region.

Belgian and Netherlands zinc coins struck during World War II were issued under the Nazi occupation. Fully brilliant specimens of these are virtually nonexistent.

In January 2002, Belgium, Luxembourg and the Netherlands replaced their currencies with coins denominated in euros, the currency of the European Union. Some coins were struck years in advance and held until 2002. On the circulating denominations, 1 cent through 2 euros, one side carries a portrait of the monarch;

the other has a common European design. On higher-denomination commemoratives, both sides are distinctively local.

Both Belgium and the Netherlands struck colonial coinages. The issues of the Belgian Congo (earlier called Congo Free State) are particularly attractive. Some are enormous copper coins; others depict a powerful elephant. Dutch colonials for the Netherlands Antilles are of homeland types, although some have a distinctive inscription. Coins for the Netherlands Indies (Indonesia today) are far more distinctive. They appear to be either European or East Asian, depending on which side one examines. Dutch colonials from World War II were struck by U.S. mints and bear their mintmarks.

Known Counterfeits: Low Countries coins have not been as extensively counterfeited as those of many other countries.

BELGIUM	VF
1919 2 Centimes, crowned A/lion with tablets (C)	.25
1916 10 Centimes (without dot after "Cent"), lion (Z)	30.00
1944 25 Centimes, monogram/three shields (Z, holed)	.20
1923 2 Francs, Belgium binding wound/caduceus (N)	2.00
1932 20 Francs, Albert/arms (N)	50.00
1934 20 Francs, similar (S)	5.00
1935 50 Francs, train station/Michael the Archangel (S)	90.00

Belgium 1935 50 Francs

Postwar Coinage	BU
1971 25 Centimes, crowned B (CN)	.25
1955 50 Centimes, large head (C)	.50
1986 5 Francs, King Baudouin (AB)	1.00
1994 5 Francs, Albert II (AB)	1.00
1960 50 Francs, king and queen/crown over two shields (S)	15.00
1989 100 Ecu, Maria Theresa (G)	1,000.00
Euro Coinage	**BU**
1999 1 Euro Cent, Albert II/globe (C-plated St.)	1.25

Belgium 1955 50 Centimes

BELGIAN CONGO	VF
1910 5 Centimes, star (CN)	1.50
1921 50 Centimes, bust l./palm tree (CN)	2.00
1926 1 Franc, Albert I./palm tree (CN)	2.75
1943 2 Francs, elephant (B, hexagonal)	6.00
1944 50 Francs, elephant (S)	50.00
RWANDA-BURUNDI	VF
1961 1 Franc, lion (B)	.50

Belgian Congo 1944 50 Francs

LUXEMBOURG	VF
1908 5 Centimes, William (CN)	1.00
1901 10 Centimes, Adolphe (CN)	.75
1924 10 Centimes, Monogram (CN)	.50
1924 2 Francs, "Ch" monogram/iron worker (N)	4.00
1929 5 Francs, Charlotte/arms at angle (S)	3.50

Postwar Coinage	BU
1970 25 Centimes, arms (AL)	.20
1957 1 Franc, "Ch" monogram/iron worker (CN)	1.25
1946 100 Francs, Jean/knight riding (S)	60.00
1964 100 Francs, Jean/arms (S)	15.00

Luxembourg 1924 10 Centimes

Luxembourg 1970 25 Centimes

NETHERLANDS (KINGDOM)	VF
1941 1 Cent, arms/value in wreath (C)	.60
1942 1 Cent, cross (Z)	.50
1941 2-1/2 Cents, arms/value in wreath (C)	2.00
1907 5 Cents, crown (CN)	6.00
1913 5 Cents, orange plant (CN, square)	3.00
1918 10 Cents, Wilhelmina as adult/wreath (S)	2.50
1939 10 Cents, Wilhelmina/wreath (S)	.75
1942 25 Cents, Viking ship (Z)	1.50
1943 25 Cents, Wilhelmina/wreath (S)	1.50
1922 1/2 Gulden, Wilhelmina/crowned shield (S)	2.50
1929 1 Gulden, Wilhelmina as adult/crowned shield (S)	3.00
1930 2-1/2 Gulden, Wilhelmina as adult/crowned shield (S)	9.00
1927 Ducat, knight standing/MO AUR REG BELGII... (G)	100.00

Netherlands 1918 10 Cents

Netherlands 1939 10 Cents

Postwar Coinage	Unc.
1948 1 Cent, Wilhelmina old (C)	3.50
1977 5 Cents, Juliana (C)	.25
1948 10 Cents, Wilhelmina old (N)	3.00
1951 25 Cents, Juliana (N)	1.50
1982 1 Gulden, Beatrix (N)	1.00
1962 2-1/2 Gulden, Juliana (S)	5.50
1999 5 Gulden, Beatrix (B-clad N)	10.00
1997 10 Gulden, Beatrix/George Marshall (S)	8.00
1982 50 Gulden, Beatrix/lion and eagle (S)	35.00
Euro Coinage	BU
2000 5 Euro Cent, Beatrix/globe (C-plated St.)	.75
2000 50 Euro Cent, Beatrix/map (B)	1.50

Netherlands 1982 50 Gulden

Netherlands 1997 10 Gulden

ARUBA	BU
1992 5 Cents, arms (N-clad St.)	.50
1995 5 Florin, Beatrix/arms (N-clad St., square)	6.00
1995 25 Florin, Beatrix/sea turtles (S)	50.00

CURACAO	VF
1944 1 Cent, lion/wreath (C)	2.00
1944 1 Gulden, Wilhelmina as adult/crowned shield (S)	12.00

NETHERLANDS ANTILLES	BU
1965 1 Cent, lion/wreath (C)	4.00
1978 25 Cents, shield (N)	1.00
1985 2-1/2 Gulden, Beatrix/arms (N)	7.00
1977 25 Gulden, Juliana/Peter Stuyvesant (S)	220.00
1978 100 Gulden, Juliana/Willem I (G)	200.00
1979 25 Gulden, children (S)	80.00

NETHERLANDS EAST INDIES	BU
1945 1 Cent, rice plant (C, holed)	2.00
1913 5 Cents, crown (CN, holed)	20.00
1945 1/4 Gulden, similar (S)	3.50

SURINAME	BU
1972 1 Cent, arms (C)	2.00
1962 1 Gulden, Juliana/arms (S)	15.00

Aruba 1995 25 Florin

Netherlands Antilles 1979 25 Gulden

Netherlands East Indies 1945 Cent

POLAND

Early modern Poland was mostly ruled by the royal house of Saxony, and its coins closely resembled German States coins of the day. Most were small coppers; small- to medium-sized coins of base silver; big, good-silver thalers; and gold. Most bore a bust, some had monograms on the obverse, and the royal arms dominated the reverse. Some of the most creative designs were on memorial issues upon the king's death. Some of these depicted a butterfly.

Poland was dissolved in 1795, but there were still Polish coins struck after that. The remnant state, the Grand Duchy of Warsaw, struck some heraldic types, though briefly. Krakow, even more briefly, did the same as an independent republic. Also, the part of Poland under Russian rule had its own distinctive coinage from 1816 to 1850. Some of these bore a portrait of the czar even when Russian coins did not. Others had the exchange rate on the reverse, giving values in both Polish and Russian currencies.

Polish independence was restored in 1918, and the crowned white eagle became a national symbol depicted on coins of the between-the-wars republic. Portraits of an idealized Polonia, an allegory of the nation, and the forceful bust of Marshall Pilsudski also were common.

After World War II, the communist government removed the crown and changed most of the minor coins to aluminum. Initially monotonous, later communist issues depict diverse national heroes and local animals. Post-communist coins are similar in style to late communist issues, but with the crown replaced on the eagle's head.

Poland has produced collector issues in quantity since the mid-1960s. The moderately priced circulating 2-zlote commemoratives, issued every few months, have proven quite popular. There is also a strong market for coins depicting Pope John Paul II.

Known Counterfeits: Counterfeits exist of the 1925 5 zlotych and klippe (square) and 1933 Sobieski 10 zlotych. An older circulation counterfeit of the 1932 5 zlotych is known.

REPUBLIC	VF
1923 10 Groszy, eagle (N)	.45
same, Nazi restrike (Z)	.20
1925 5 Zlotych, eagle/Polonia and youth (S)	350.00
1936 5 Zlotych, Pilsudski/eagle (S)	5.00
1925 20 Zlotych, King Boleslaus/eagle (G)	400.00 BU

Poland 1936 5 Zlotych

Postwar Coinage	BU
1949 5 Groszy, eagle (C)	1.50
1958 5 Groszy, eagle (AL)	.25
1962 5 Groszy, eagle (AL)	.25
1960 5 Zlotych, eagle/fisher (AL)	6.00
1967 10 Zlotych, eagle/Marie Curie (CN)	3.00
1978 100 Zlotych, moose/eagle (S), PF	30.00
1991 20,000 Zlotych, SAR monogram/eagle (CN in B)	22.00
1992 5 Groszy, crowned eagle (B)	.45
1997 2 Zlote, beetle/crowned eagle (B)	25.00
1997 10 Zlotych, Pope with Eucharist/similar (S), PF	45.00

Poland 1978 100 Zlotych

Poland 1992 5 Groszy

PORTUGAL

Twentieth-century Portuguese coinage, both circulating and commemorative, emphasizes the country's nautical heritage.

In January 2002, Portugal replaced the escudo with coins denominated in euros, the currency of the European Union. On the circulating denominations, 1 cent through 2 euros, one side carries a Portuguese design, the other a common European design. On higher-denomination commemoratives, both sides are distinctively Portuguese.

During the 1600s, much Portuguese silver was revalued by the application of a countermark with a new value.

Portugal maintained its colonial empire longer than most European powers and had an extensive colonial coinage. During the 1600s and 1700s, most of it was either homeland types or it bore a globe on the reverse. The coins of Portuguese India, up to the 1800s, are interesting for their European designs combined with primitive methods of local manufacture. Early in the 20th century, Portugal's colonial coinage was fairly uniform from colony to colony. By the 1930s, a distinctive formula was developed: One side bore an emblem of Portugal, the other a heraldic symbol of the colony itself. On smaller denominations, one of these was sometimes replaced by the value.

KINGDOM (MANUEL II, 1908-1910)	VF
1909 200 Reis, head l./crown in wreath (S)	6.50
1910 500 Reis, Emanuel II/winged Victory (S)	25.00

REPUBLIC	XF
1918 2 Centavos, arms (C)	2.00
same but iron	300.00
1919 4 Centavos, bust of young girl (CN)	1.75
1916 50 Centavos, bust/armellary sphere (S)	10.00
1910 Escudo, bust with torch/arms (S)	200.00
1933 5 Escudos, ship/arms (S)	20.00
1942 5 Escudos, same	9.00
1948 5 Escudos, same	5.00
1934 10 Escudos, similar (S)	50.00

REPUBLIC	BU
1968 20 Centavos, cross of shields/XX (C)	2.00
1983 2-1/2 Escudos, corn ear/arms (CN)	1.50
1966 20 Escudos, bridge/arms (S)	7.00
1986 50 Escudos, sailboat/arms (CN)	2.75
1991 100 Escudos, de Quental (CN)	5.00
1997 200 Escudos, Francis Xavier/ship (CN)	6.00

Portugal 1916 50 Centavos

Portugal 1942 5 Escudos

Portugal 1966 20 Escudos

ANGOLA	VF
1921 1 Centavo, arms (C)	20.00
1927 10 Centavos, bust l./arms (CN)	4.00
1953 1 Escudo (C)	1.50
1952 10 Escudos, Portuguese arms/Angolan arms (S)	2.50
1972 20 Escudos, Portuguese arms/Angolan arms (N)	2.50
AZORES	VF
1901 5 Reis, arms/wreath (C)	3.50
1980 25 Escudos, arms (CN)	7.50 BU

Angola 1927 10 Centavos

CAPE VERDE	XF
1930 5 Centavos (C)	3.50
1930 10 Centavos, head l. (C)	4.00
1949 50 Centavos, arms (CN)	2.50
1967 2-1/2 Escudos, Portuguese arms/Cape Verde arms (CN)	2.50
1953 10 Escudos, similar (S)	6.50

Cape Verde 1930 5 Centavos

Cape Verde 1953 10 Escudos

PORTUGUESE GUINEA	XF
1933 10 Centavos, head l. (C)	500.00
1946 50 Centavos, arms (C)	15.00
1952 2-1/2 Escudos, Portuguese arms/Guinea arms (CN)	3.00
1973 5 Escudos, similar (CN)	10.00
1952 20 Escudos, similar (S)	45.00
PORTUGUESE INDIA	**VF**
1901 1/4 Tanga, Carlos I/arms (C)	16.00
1934 2 Tangas, Indian shield/Portuguese shield (CN)	20.00
1935 Rupia, Portuguese shield/Indian shield (S)	15.00
1961 10 Centavos, arms (C)	1.00
1958 1 Escudo, Portuguese arms/Indian arms (CN)	2.50
1959 6 Escudos, similar (CN)	4.50

Portuguese India 1935 Rupia

MACAO	BU
1952 5 Avos, arms (C)	50.00
1973 50 Avos, Portuguese arms/Macao arms (CN)	5.00
1952 1 Pataca, similar (S)	50.00
1998 2 Patacas, church and gateway (NB, octagonal)	5.50
1992 5 Patacas, junk passing cathedral (CN, 12-sided)	10.00
1989 100 Patacas, arms/snake (S)	60.00

Macao 1952 5 Avos

Macao 1992 5 Patacas

Macao 1989 100 Patacas

MADEIRA ISLANDS	BU

1981 25 Escudos, head of Zarco/arms (CN)   9.00

Madeira Islands 1981 25 Escudos

MOZAMBIQUE	VF
1936 10 Centavos, arms (C)	10.00
1945 50 Centavos, arms (C)	3.50
1951 1 Escudo, arms (CN)	3.00
1965 2-1/2 Escudos, Portuguese arms/Mozambique arms (CN)	.25
1935 5 Escudos, similar (S)	22.50
1960 5 Escudos, similar (S)	2.25
1970 10 Escudos, similar (CN)	.70
1955 20 Escudos, similar (S)	5.00

Mozambique 1970 10 Escudos

ST. THOMAS AND PRINCE ISLAND	VF
1971 10 Centavos, arms (AL)	.65
1962 20 Centavos, arms (C)	1.25
1951 50 Centavos, arms (CN)	3.50
1948 1 Escudo, arms (N-C)	40.00
1939 2-1/2 Escudos, Portuguese arms/colonial arms (S)	30.00
1951 5 Escudos, similar (S)	7.00
1951 10 Escudos, similar (S)	9.00
	BU
1971 20 Escudos, similar (N)	15.00
1970 50 Escudos, two shields/cross of shields (S)	10.00

St. Thomas and Prince Island 1962 20 Centavos

TIMOR	XF
1951 10 Avos, cross of shields (C)	7.50
1945 20 Avos, bust r./arms (CN)	70.00
1951 50 Avos, arms (S)	9.00
1970 20 Centavos, arms (C)	2.50
1970 1 Escudo, arms (C)	7.00
1970 2-1/2 Escudos, Portuguese arms/Timor arms (CN)	3.50
1958 3 Escudos, similar (S)	10.00
1970 5 Escudos, similar (CN)	6.50
1958 6 Escudos (S), similar (S)	12.50

Timor 1945 20 Avos

RUSSIA

Russia has the dual distinction of being the last European country to abandon primitive medieval-hammered coinage and the first with a modern decimal-based coinage. When the silver-dollar-sized rouble was introduced in 1704, it was valued at 100 of the old kopeks. Modern Russian coinage is attributed to the personal will of Peter the Great, who was determined to make Russia a modern country in his lifetime. Before his reign, portrait coins were virtually unheard of in Russia, and large silver or gold coins were generally imported. He was also the first ruler since the 1400s to successfully circulate copper coinage.

The standards of copper coins changed several times in the 1700s and 1800s, and often, new coins were struck over old ones. Specialized collectors consider these particularly desirable, but not everyone cares.

During the early and mid-1800s, portraiture was removed from silver coinage. It was replaced by a double-headed eagle. Throughout the century, the number of shields on its wings increased. Each shield represented an additional territory, such as Finland or Poland, that the czar had incorporated into his empire.

One distinctive type of coin struck under czarist Russia is the novodel. This is an official government "restrike" with new dies. Some novodels are actually new issues of old coins that were never struck. They can sometimes be identified by their unusually uniform quality, not representative of the earlier coins they resemble. They were generally struck for wealthy 19th-century collectors and today are considered rare and desirable.

From 1921-23, coins were struck in the name of the Russian Soviet Federated Socialist Republic. These pieces carried the communist slogan "Workers of all countries unite!" and agricultural symbols. With the establishment of the Union of Soviet Socialist Republics and the addition of new territories, symbols of expansion appeared. The new state symbol consisted of a hammer and sickle superimposed on a globe with ribbons at its side. Each ribbon represented a republic added to the Soviet Union, much as the shields were added to the czarist eagle's wings. Among the most splendid depictions of Soviet iconography is the scene on the Soviet rouble of 1924. Nicknamed the "worker rouble," it shows an industrial worker pointing out the rising sun of communism to a less enthusiastic agricultural worker. This relates clearly to the difficulties implicit in Russia, an agrarian nation, being the first to implement communism, a system originally intended for an industrial society.

During the 1970s and 1980s, a wide range of commemoratives was released. Some base-metal pieces were widely distributed in the Soviet Union; others, mostly platinum or silver, were not available to the average Soviet citizen. Much of the commemorative coin program continued after the fall of communism, but other changes occurred. Most of the low-value circulating coins released over the last several years bear the double-headed eagle, former symbol of czarist Russia, for the first time since 1918. Another post-communist phenomenon was rapid inflation. This has caused a revaluation of the currency, followed by more inflation.

After the fall of communism, the republics within the USSR became independent nations. Among the most important, besides Russia proper, is the Ukraine. Ukrainian coins were released after years of being distributed unofficially in small quantities. Because of the initial difficulty in obtaining them, followed by abundant supplies, Ukrainian minor coinage has been the subject of one of the most precipitous drops in value in the recent world numismatic market. The trident symbol depicted on them goes back to the early coinage of Kievian Rus, virtually all of which are considered museum pieces.

Known Counterfeits: Many new counterfeits of czarist coins have appeared recently.

NICHOLAS II, 1894-1917	VF
1909 1/2 Kopek, crowned "NII" monogram (C)	5.00
1903 3 Kopeks, two-headed eagle in ornate border/wreath (C)	6.00
1905 5 Kopeks, two-headed eagle/wreath (S)	8.00
1902 5 Roubles, similar (G)	280.00
1902 37-1/2 Roubles, similar (CN)	25.00 Unc.

1902 37-1/2 Roubles, similar (CN)
This is a restrike with original dies. Look for the "P" added after 1902a. Beware: Some have been gold plated.

COMMUNIST RUSSIA (PCACP)	XF
1923 10 Kopeks, hammer and sickle/wreath (S)	10.00
1923 20 Kopeks, similar (S)	12.00
1921 50 Kopeks, similar/star (S)	30.00

SOVIET UNION (CCCP)	XF
1925 1/2 Kopek, CCCP (C)	40.00
1931 1 Kopek, arms/wreath (ALB)	4.00
1936 2 Kopeks, similar (ALB)	5.00
1943 3 Kopeks, similar (ALB)	3.00
1952 5 Kopeks, similar (ALB)	4.00
1957 10 Kopeks, arms/octagon (CN)	4.00
1965 15 Kopeks, arms (CNZ)	4.00
1967 20 Kopeks, arms/ship (CNZ)	2.00
1991 50 Kopeks, dome and tower (CN)	2.00
1924 Rouble, industrial worker leading farmer toward sun/arms (S)	70.00

SOVIET UNION (CCCP)	BU
1981 Rouble, cosmonaut/arms (CN)	4.00
1991 5 Roubles, cathedral/arms (CN)	7.00
1979 150 Roubles, wrestlers/arms (platinum)	900.00

Soviet Union (CCCP) 1924 Rouble

Soviet Union (CCCP) 1979 150 Roubles

RUSSIAN FEDERATION	BU
1992 1 Rouble, two-headed eagle (B-clad St.)	3.00
1994 50 Roubles, flamingos/two-headed eagle (ALB in CN)	9.00
1995 100 Roubles, ballerina/similar (G), PF	695.00

UKRAINE	BU
1996 200,000 Karbovantsiv, Chernobyl memorial, bell/arms (CN)	8.00
1993 2 Kopiyky, arms/value (AL)	1.50
2000 5 Hryven, Christ, crowds in background/arms between two angels (CNZ)	15.00

Ukraine 1993 2 Kopiyky

SCANDINAVIA

Scandinavian coins first became common in the 1500s. By the 1600s, the small base-silver coins of Denmark were frequently found. During this period, the coins of Sweden and Denmark follow a typical European pattern of portraits, monograms, crowns, and shields. Other features are distinctive. In both countries, standing figures of the monarch become more common than elsewhere in Europe. Monograms in Denmark are more likely to use modern numerals rather than Roman numerals. In Sweden, the divine name, the Tetragramaton, in Hebrew is often depicted.

The single most distinguishing feature of Scandinavian coinage is the abundant use of copper. Large copper coins struck on crudely made blanks were common, particularly in 1600s Sweden. Also, large slabs of copper, called "plate money," were used instead of silver coins. Each piece, weighing up to several pounds, was usually stamped five times with circular dies: once in each corner to prevent clipping and once in the center. Most of the plate money on the market in recent years is from one shipwreck, the Nicobar, and is corroded. These are worth less than non-sea-salvaged pieces. By the late 1700s, plate money had ceased to be struck, but large copper continued to be common throughout Scandinavia.

During the 1800s, Scandinavian coins were decimalized, and in 1872, a common monetary union was formed, with all Scandinavian countries striking distinctive coins on a common standard. During this time, most countries used portraits only on silver and gold, and monograms on copper.

Norway has been part of either the Danish (1397-1814) or the Swedish (1814-1905) monarchy through most of the modern era. In 1905, it elected its own king, Haakon VII. Modern Norwegian coins usually reflected the kingdom with which it was united—sometimes with the distinctive Norwegian arms, a lion with a battle ax, and other times differentiated only by a small crossed-hammers mintmark.

Iceland had no separate coinage until 1922, Greenland until 1926. Before then, Danish coins circulated on both islands. In 1941, Iceland became independent, and royal symbols, such as the crown, were removed from above the arms. Many recent coins show the guardian spirits of Iceland, sometimes supporting the country's shield. After 1964, regular Danish coins were reintroduced to Greenland, and today it is an integral part of Denmark.

All of these countries have issued plentiful silver commemoratives in the modern era, with some base-metal ones more recently.

One convenient way to distinguish Swedish coins from other Scandinavian coins is that the word ore is spelled with ö in Swedish, ø in the others.

Following are the names of the Scandinavian countries in their native languages:

Denmark	DANMARK
Greenland	GRØNLAND
Iceland	ISLAND
Norway	NORGE or NOREG
Sweden	SVERIGE

Denmark struck colonial coins for its possessions in the West Indies. They are generally artistic and not particularly rare. In 1913, Denmark sold these islands to the United States and they became the U.S. Virgin Islands. Today, these coins are popular with collectors of Danish and U.S. coins alike. The coins of Danish India are scarcer and less popular.

DENMARK	VF
1907 2 Øre, crowned F8 monogram (C)	3.00
1919 5 Øre, crowned Cx monogram (C)	5.50
1924 25 Øre, crowned CxR (CN, holed)	1.75
1942 25 Øre, similar (Z, holed)	3.50
1925 1/2 Krone, crowned CxC monogram/crown (ALB)	9.00
1923 2 Kroner, king and queen/arms (S)	15.00
	BU
1908 10 Kroner, Frederik VIII/arms (G)	325.00
1913 10 Kroner, Frederick VII/arms (G)	325.00
Postwar Coinage	**BU**
1962 1 Øre, crowned FRIX monogram (Z)	2.00
1973 10 Øre, crowned M2R monogram (CN)	.50
1957 1 Krone, Frederick XI/shield (ALB)	5.00
1968 10 Kroner, Frederick XI/Princess Benedikte (S)	60.00
1992 200 Kroner, queen and prince/stylized house (S)	60.00

Denmark 1992 200 Kroner

GREENLAND	XF
1926 25 Øre, crowned shield/bear (CN)	15.00
same but holed	90.00
1960 1 Krone, crown over two shields/wreath (CN)	12.50

ICELAND	XF
1931 1 Eyrir, crowned Cx (C)	6.00
1942 2 Aurar, similar (C)	1.00
1963 5 Aurar, shield in wreath (C)	.75
1981 10 Aurar, ox/cuttle-fish (C)	1.00 BU
1922 25 Aurar, crowned shield (CN)	4.00
1940 1 Krona, similar (ALB)	5.00

	BU
1981 1 Krona, giant/cod (CN)	1.50
1970 10 Kronur, arms (CN)	1.00
1987 50 Kronur, four spirits/crab (NB)	6.00
1995 100 Kronur, same/lumpfish (NB)	12.00
1974 500 Kronur, four spirits/woman leading cow (S)	16.00
2000 1,000 Kronur, Leif Ericson (S), PF	75.00

This was sold in a two-piece set with the United States Leif Ericson commemorative.

Iceland 1974 500 Kronur

NORWAY	VF
1917 10 Øre, crowned H7 monogram (billon)	3.00
1939 50 Øre, cross of monograms/crown (CN, holed)	.60
1906 2 Kroner, arms/tree within border of hands (S)	70.00

Postwar Coinage	BU
1957 1 Øre, crowned H7 monogram (C)	3.25
1964 10 Øre, crowned Ov monogram/bee (CN)	1.35
1992 1 Krone, Harald V/crown (CN)	.65
1964 10 Kroner, arms/building (S)	11.50

Norway 1906 2 Kroner

Norway 1964 10 Kroner

Norway 1993 100 Kroner

SWEDEN	VF
1920 1 Öre, crowned GvG monogram/three crowns (C)	.50
1935 same (C)	.30
1917 2 Öre, crowned GvG monogram/three crowns (iron)	3.00
1904 5 Öre, crowned OII monogram (C)	2.00
1941 5 Öre, crowned GvG monogram/three crowns (C)	.35
1934 10 Öre, crowned shield (billon)	.50
1943 25 Öre, crown (billon)	.50
1907 50 Öre, crowned OII monogram/wreath (S)	5.00
1938 50 Öre, crowned shield (S)	1.50
1940 50 Öre, crowned Gv monogram/wreath (CN)	1.00
1936 1 Krona, Gustaf V/arms (S)	2.50
1944 2 Kronor, Gustaf V old/arms (billon)	3.00
	Unc.
1953 1 Öre, crown/crown (C)	2.00
1967 2 Öre, similar (C)	.45
1979 5 Öre, crowned CXVIG monogram (C-tin-Z)	.30
1988 10 Öre, similar (CN)	.15
1956 25 Öre, crown (billon)	3.50
1968 50 Öre, crowned GVIA monogram (CN)	1.25
1979 1 Krona, Carl XVI/crowned shield (CN-clad C)	.75

Sweden 1904 5 Öre

SWEDEN	Unc.
1964 2 Kronor, Gustaf VI/crowned shield (billon)	4.50
1952 5 Kronor, Gustaf VI/crowned GVIA monogram (billon)	30.00
1972 10 Kronor, Gustaf VI/signature (S)	9.50
1976 50 Kronor, King and queen/arms (S)	14.50
1990 200 Kronor, Carl XVI/ship Vasa (S)	35.00
1993 200 Kronor, 20th anniversary Carl XVI (S)	35.00
1993 1,000 Kronor, queen/arms (G)	185.00

Sweden 1952 5 Kronor

Sweden 1967 2 Öre

Sweden 1990 200 Kronor

Sweden 1979 5 Öre

SPAIN

During the 1500s through early 1800s, Spanish coins were among the most important international trade coins in the world, particularly those struck at Spain's colonial mints in the Americas. They were so respected that they were the standard of value on which the original U.S. dollar was based.

Until the mid-1800s, Spanish coinage was based on the real introduced by Ferdinand and Isabella. It was originally a silver coin larger than a quarter, although it had shrunk to the size of a nickel and was thinner by the 1600s. From then until the Napoleonic Wars, it remained quite stable. During most of this period, it carried the Spanish coat of arms on the reverse, a portrait or variation of the arms on the obverse.

Gold coins were plentiful as well. They were denominated in escudos, worth 16 reales. They bore portraits more often than the silver did.

Copper coins were denominated in maravedi, 34 of which were worth one real. During most of this period, the copper coinage was poor. There was often a shortage of new copper, causing old, worn-out coins to continue in use long after they should have been replaced. Often these coins were counterstamped to revalidate them. A number indicating a new value and sometimes a date was impressed. When this was done repeatedly, the coins took on a mutilated appearance, and sometimes ceased to remain flat. This practice of making resellados ended in the 1700s, but the practice of forcing worn-out copper into continued use persisted.

Spanish coins from the mid-1800s until recently have carried two dates. The large date is the year of authorization, not the date of manufacture. The real date was usually indicated in tiny incuse numbers on the six-pointed star, which is a Madrid mintmark.

After a few monetary experiments in the mid-1800s, Spain joined many other European countries in 1869 in striking its coins according to the international standard of the Latin Monetary Union and continued to do so until 1926. Most of the issues during this period uniformly bore the royal portrait and the coat of arms.

The final years of the monarchy and the civil war not only saw a deterioration of the coinage's value but also new design ideas under all three governments. Despite the modernistic eagle supporting the shield, Franco's later coinage, mostly of base metal, was fairly conservative in pattern.

The restoration of the monarchy not only promised a progressive government for Spain but also changes in the coinage. Since the 1980s, new shapes have been used to distinguish denominations, and a plethora of designs have been used to promote the recognition of various cultural sights and events throughout Spain. There have also been a vast number of collector issues sold at a premium. These, too, have had unusual and progressive designs.

In January 2002, Spain replaced the peseta with coins denominated in euros, the currency of the European Union.

Some coins were struck years in advance and held until 2002. On the circulating denominations, 1 cent through 2 euros, one side carries a Spanish design, the other a common European design. On higher-denomination commemoratives, both sides are distinctively Spanish.

COLONIAL COINAGE

The real issued in the New World was struck to the same standards as in European Spain, but the designs often varied. The first issues of the early 1500s displayed the Pillars of Hercules and a coat of arms. In terms of style, they seemed no different from European coins. The first copper coins struck in the New World, minted in Santo Domingo, featured monograms, but they were far more carelessly made.

When the quantities of silver and gold being mined and shipped back to Spain became so great that they could not be struck into nicely finished coins, a rough, improvised coin was devised. Called "cobs" by modern collectors, these coins were struck to the same exacting weight standards, but the designs were only hastily impressed, with no entire image being found on any one coin. The blanks on which they were struck were neither round nor flat. Originally, it was intended that these be shipped back to Europe and melted, but the pressing needs for money in the Spanish American colonies caused them to be pressed into service as regular coinage.

Dates were engraved on the dies of these cobs, but they are usually not clear on the coins. Specialized references sometimes permit the dating of these pieces by the correlation of mintmarks and assayers' initials, which are usually more legible than the dates.

Many of the cobs on the market were recovered from shipwrecks or found on beaches near shipwrecks. Generally, sea-salvaged coins are either pitted or covered with black compounds called horn silver. This is bonded to the metal and cannot be removed without removing part of the coin. Such corroded coins are worth far less than other cobs and Spanish colonial coins. The exceptions are coins with pedigrees known to shipwrecks. If satisfactorily documented, the novelty value of their history can far exceed their value as low-grade Spanish colonial coins. Be careful of false documentation and made-to-order pedigrees. When possible, documentation from the original salvagers is desirable.

From 1732 onward, more careful methods of manufacture were implemented. Initially, the improved silver carried the crowned shield of Spain on one side and two globes between the Pillars of Hercules on the other. In 1760, the designs were changed to bear the king's portrait and a Spanish shield. The face value of each silver coin was indicated in numbers of reales, 8R through 1R, with the half real simply as "R" without a numeral. The improved gold had carried a similar design since the 1730s. Copper in the Spanish colonies was not common and was not struck at most mints.

REPUBLIC & CIVIL WAR	VF
1938 10 Centimos, arms (iron)	600.00
1937 25 Centimos, yoke and arrows/crowned shield (CN, holed)	.40
1937 1 Peseta, head l./grapes (B)	.85

FRANCO REGENCY	BU
1953 10 Centimos, horseman/arms (AL)	8.00
1959 10 Centimos, Franco (AL)	.35
1966 1 Peseta, Franco/arms (ALB)	4.50
1949 5 Pesetas, similar (N)	10.00
1957 25 Pesetas, Franco/eagle holding arms (CN)	3.00
1966 100 Pesetas, Franco/arms in octolobe (S)	11.00

Spain 1959 10 Centimos

KINGDOM RESTORED	BU
1983 1 Peseta, Juan Carlos/arms (AL)	.75
1990 50 Pesetas, Juan Carlos/globe (CN, notched)	1.50
1994 100 Pesetas, Juan Carlos/Prado Museum (NB)	3.50
1989 5,000 Pesetas, arms/ship Santa Maria (S)	45.00
1999 2,000 Pesetas, train (S), PF	32.50
EURO COINAGE	BU
1999 20 Euro Cent, Cervantes/map (B, notched)	1.00
2000 1 Euro, Juan Carlos/map (CN-clad N in NB)	4.50

Spain 1983 Peseta

Spain 1999 2,000 Pesetas

SWITZERLAND

While the Swiss cantons (provinces) gradually formed a union during the 13th through 15th centuries, each one maintained its own coinage. During the early modern period, most had a range of small silver denominations, with some striking silver-dollar-sized talers and gold. Copper was not generally favored, so small denominations were usually struck in billon, a very base silver-copper alloy.

During the Napoleonic era, a Swiss republic was established (1798-1803), and even after its demise, the various cantons maintained similar standards. After a Swiss confederation was founded, a uniform national coinage was created, replacing the issues of the cantons in 1850. It was based on the French franc, which became an international standard under the Latin Monetary Union.

Shooting competitions have been major events for centuries in Switzerland. Many of these festivities were commemorated, especially in the 19th century, by special silver talers and later 5-franc pieces of high artistic merit. These are much prized by collectors and should be examined carefully for signs of cleaning, which reduces their value.

The regular coinage of Switzerland is perhaps the most conservative in the world, reflecting its stability and resistance to inflation. Bearing a female representation of Helvetia, the allegory of the nation, or the Swiss cross, the designs of many denominations have not changed in more than 125 years. Like most countries, Switzerland moved from silver to base metal in 1968. Interestingly, Swiss coins rarely bear any language spoken in Switzerland. Because of the awkwardness of inscribing the coins in the four different languages spoken there, most coins are inscribed only in Latin. Switzerland in Latin is Helvetia, Swiss is Helvetica.

Known Counterfeits: Gold 20 francs of the late 19th and 20th centuries should be examined with reasonable care. A partial list of years counterfeited include 1897, 1900, 1902-04, 1911, 1912, 1915, 1919, 1922, 1927, 1930, 1931, 1933, and 1935, all with the B mintmark. The 1935 with the LB mintmark is an official restrike from 1945-47.

Switzerland 1920 20 Rappen

CONFEDERATION	VF
1910 1 Rappen, same (C)	15.00
1942 5 Rappen, head of Helvetia (CN)	.25
1907 20 Rappen, head of Helvetia (N)	1.00
1920 20 Rappen, same (N)	.50
1906 1/2 Franc, Helvetia standing/wreath (S)	3.00
1907 1 Franc, similar (S)	3.50
1939 2 Francs, similar (S)	5.00
1931 5 Francs, William Tell/shield (S)	50.00
1950 5 Francs, William Tell/shield (S)	10.00

	Unc.
1963 2 Rappen, cross/wheat ear (C)	1.50
1993 5 Rappen, head of Helvetia/wreath (AL-B)	.50
1956 1 Franc, Helvetia standing/wreath (S)	6.50
1967 1 Franc, Helvetia standing/wreath (S)	6.00
1963 5 Francs, Red Cross commemorative, nurse and patients in form of cross (S)	15.00
1984 5 Francs, high altitude balloon and deep-water submarine (CN)	8.00
1922 10 Francs, bust of Helvetia/radiant cross (G)	95.00

Switzerland 1956 Franc

Switzerland 1950 5 Francs

Switzerland 1963 5 Francs

Switzerland 1984 5 Francs

AFRICAN COINS

Coinage largely did not come to sub-Saharan Africa until the colonial era, when Europeans introduced it extensively for their territories, which at first lay along the coast and later stretched inland. There were, however, some earlier exceptions. The most important and distinctive coinage of early sub-Saharan Africa was that of the ancient kingdom of Axum, located in present-day Ethiopia.

Beginning in about 270 and continuing as late as about 640, the coins of this African monarchy were small but were struck in all three classic metals: gold, silver and bronze. Their most unusual and impressive feature was the use of a gold inlay on many of the bronze coins. Sometimes this was just a dot in the center, other times a large area surrounding the king's bust. When intact, these inlays are dramatic.

Another notable feature of Axumite coinage is the first use of Christian symbolism as the design's primary motif. The cross became quite common on these pieces. Also of interest was the use of Ge'ez, the distinctive Axumite alphabet, which today has the distinction of being the alphabet frequently used in Ethiopia for liturgical purposes.

Just because coins came late to Africa does not mean the region did without currency. Many distinctive forms of exchange existed, and they are today a collecting field unique to itself.

Broadly speaking, three of the most common categories of this money were cowries, beads and metal objects of various forms. Cowrie shells constitute a primitive form of currency common to most continents. They were traded in Asia, the Pacific, and the Americas. Later, they were replaced or supplemented by manufactured beads.

Trade beads were used as early as the 1400s in Niger, where they were made of terra cotta. Later, more elaborate designs evolved in glass, simpler ones occasionally in stone. Many were made locally, and as trade with Europe expanded, more were imported.

By far the most famous currency of Africa is that of bronze and iron. The "kissie" or "Ghizzi" penny was popular among the Kissi, Bandi, Gbandia, Gola, Kpelle, Loma, Mandingo, and Mendi tribes living in the areas of modern Guinea, Liberia and Sierra Leone. Used from the 1880s to the 1930s, they consisted of twisted rods of iron about 9 to 15 inches long. One end was formed into a "T" and the other a paddle. Its strange shape ultimately derives from a hoe.

Another famous African metal trade currency was the various crosses of central Africa. Small H-shaped ingots and medium to large X-shaped ingots of copper were traded in Zambia and Katanga during the 1700s and 1800s.

A third class of metal trade goods was the bracelet. It was originally of African manufacture, but Europeans quickly learned the utility of arriving with acceptable local currency. Today, most of the smaller late forms of these "manillas" are believed to have been cast in Birmingham.

The first sub-Saharan countries to strike their own modern coins were, logically, the only two to avoid European colonization: Ethiopia and Liberia. Ethiopia's first modern coins were struck by King Menelik II, who unified the country in the 1880s. Though there had long been a royal dynasty in Ethiopia, traditionally descended from the biblical King Solomon, actual power had been divided between local feudal princes before Menelik's reign.

The other country to strike early independent coinage, Liberia, was founded in 1822 as a refuge for freed American slaves. The first Liberian cents of 1833 were distinctive in their design, but later issues depicting a Liberty head looked more like U.S. patterns than African coins. It was, in fact, not until 1960 that Liberty took on African instead of European facial features.

A third independent African country, although not native in culture, also began issuing coins in 1874. This was the Dutch Zuid Afrikaansche Republiek (the Transvaal). Its coinage was short-lived, however, as the country was conquered by the British during the Boer War and incorporated into their empire in 1902.

Beginning in 1957, and finally completed in 1975, African countries gained their independence from the colonial powers. Most wasted little time in emphasizing their independence by exercising the sovereign prerogative of striking coins. Those new states not finding it useful to strike coins in quantity to circulate in commerce, at the very least, struck them in limited numbers for presentation and commemorative purposes.

It is not unusual for central and west African countries not to strike their own coins for circulation. Many of these states have found benefit in belonging to one of two currency unions. A common currency throughout every country in such a union facilitates trade and economic stability.

The most common obverse design on new African coinages was the portrait of a founding statesman. The coat of arms was also a common obverse and, when it was not used for that, often found its way onto the reverse. One of the most common motifs, however, is the wonderful proliferation of exotic animals that have graced African coins since the 1960s. Such devices have made even the circulation strikes of Africa popular with collectors worldwide.

Most of the precious-metal coins of post-colonial Africa are struck solely for sale to collectors, and many are struck only in proof. Recently, countries such as Liberia and Somaliland, both caught in protracted civil wars, have started striking small denominations for export to collectors as well.

Known Counterfeits: The most commonly counterfeited African coins are the gold coins of Axum and to an extent those in other metals. The most commonly counterfeited modern African coin is the gold Krugerrand of South Africa. Fraudulent pieces have been common since the 1970s, often cast, some with real gold shells around a tungsten core.

ANGOLA	Unc.
1978 1 Kwanza, arms (CN)	1.50
(1977) 10 Kwanzas, arms (CN)	3.50
1999 50 Centimos, arms (C-plated St.)	1.00

Angola 1999 50 Centimos

BENIN (DAHOMEY)	Unc.
1971 1,000 Francs, Somba woman/arms (S), PF	150.00
1994 200 Francs, Tyrannosaurus Rex/arms (C)	30.00

Benin (Dahomey) 1994 200 Francs

BOTSWANA	Unc.
1966 50 Cents, Seretse Khama/arms (S)	7.00
1991 1 Thebe, arms/head of Turako bird (AL)	.40

Botswana 1966 50 Cents

BURUNDI	Unc.
1965 1 Franc, arms (B)	3.00
1993 1 Franc, arms (AL)	1.50
1965 10 Francs, King Mwanbutsa/arms (G)	90.00
1968 10 Francs, grain and bananas (CN)	3.50

Burundi 1968 10 Francs

CENTRAL AFRICAN STATES	Unc.
1978 1 Franc, three giant eland (AL)	2.00
1973 5 Francs, similar (AL-B)	1.65
1992 100 Francs, similar (N)	4.50

CHAD	Unc.
1970 100 Francs, Africa/Robert F. Kennedy (S), PF	75.00
1985 100 Francs, three giant eland (N)	30.00
1999 1,000 Francs, Galileo (S), PF	30.00

PEOPLE'S REPUBLIC OF CONGO	Unc.
1990 100 Francs, three giant eland (N)	6.00
1993 100 Francs, woman inscribing tablet/sailing ship (CN)	10.00
1996 500 Francs, same/lion head (S), PF	40.00

CONGO, DEMOCRATIC REPUBLIC (ZAIRE)	Unc.
1965 10 Francs, lion face (AL)	7.00
1987 1 Zaire, President Mobutu (B)	2.00
1971 50 Zaires, same/Hotel Intercontinental (G), PF	1,325.00

People's Republic of Congo 1996 500 Francs

DJIBOUTI	Unc.
1977 1 Franc, arms/antelope bust (AL)	3.00
1991 100 Francs, arms/camels (CN)	7.50

Djibouti 1977 Franc

EQUATORIAL AFRICAN STATES	Unc.
1990 1 Franc, three giant eland (AL)	2.00
1982 25 Francs, similar (ALB)	2.50
1977 500 Francs, woman r./stylized eland (CN)	16.50
EQUATORIAL GUINEA	**Unc.**
1969 1 Peseta, tusks/arms (ALB)	2.50
1970 75 Pesetas, Lenin (S), PF	21.50
1970 100 Pesetas, arms and tusks/naked Maja (S), PF	35.00
1985 5 Francos, three eland (ALB)	8.00

Equatorial Guinea 1970 75 Pesetas

ERITREA	Unc.
1997 1 Cent, soldiers with flag/antelope (N-clad St.)	.50
1997 25 Cents, same/zebra (N-clad St.)	1.25
1994 1 Dollar, arms/cheetah (CN)	14.00

ETHIOPIA	Unc.
1923 1 Werk, Empress Zauditu/lion (G)	750.00
1923 50 Matonas, Haile Selassie crowned/lion (N)	3.00
1936 1 Cent, Haile Selassie/lion (C)	1.00
1936 25 Cents, similar (C, scalloped and reeded)	4.00
1972 5 Dollars, similar (S), PF	25.00
1964 100 Dollars, similar (G), PF	1,150.00
1977 10 Cents, lion head/antelope (C-Z)	1.50
1974 2 Birr, lion head/two soccer players (CN)	12.00
1998 20 Birr, children (S), PF	50.00

Ethiopia 1972 5 Dollars

GABON	Unc.
1960 10 Francs, Leon Mba/arms (G), PF	125.00
1985 100 Francs, three giant eland (N)	10.00

Gabon 1985 100 Francs

GAMBIA	Unc.
1971 1 Butut, bust/peanuts (C)	.20
1971 1 Dalasi, bust/crocodile (CN)	8.00
1987 1 Dalasi, similar (CN, heptagonal)	6.00
1996 1 Dalasi, arms/three kings (CN)	16.50
1977 40 Dalasis, bust/aardvark (S)	25.00

Gambia 1996 Dalasi

GHANA	Unc.
1958 3 Pence, Kwame Nkrumah/star (CN, scalloped)	1.00
1958 10 Shillings, same (S), PF	17.50
1967 5 Pesewas, cocoa beans/arms (CN)	.75
1991 20 Cedis, cowrie/arms (N-clad St.)	1.50
1986 100 Cedis, drums/Commonwealth Games (S)	16.50
GUINEA	Unc.
1959 10 Francs, Ahmed Sekou Toure (ALB)	90.00
1962 1 Franc, similar (CN)	7.00
1971 1 Syli, bust l. (AL)	12.50
1985 5 Francs, arms/palm branch (B-clad St.)	1.00
1988 100 Francs, arms/discus thrower (S)	75.00

Guinea 1959 10 Francs

GUINEA-BISSAU	Unc.
1977 50 Centavos, arms/palm tree (AL)	8.00
(1995) 2,000 Pesos, arms/agricultural scenes (N-plated St.)	17.50

Guinea-Bissau (1995) 2,000 Pesos

Ivory Coast 1966 10 Francs

IVORY COAST	PF
1966 10 Francs, President Boigny/elephant (S)	50.00
similar but gold	90.00

KATANGA	Unc.
1961 1 Franc, bananas/Katanga cross (C)	4.00

KENYA	Unc.
1966 5 Cents, Jomo Kenyatta/arms (N-B)	1.00
1969 10 Cents, similar but legend around bust (N-B)	1.00
1975 50 Cents, similar (CN)	1.00
1980 1 Shilling, Daniel Arap Moi/arms (CN)	1.50
1994 10 Shillings, similar (B around CN)	6.00
1991 1,000 Shillings, similar (S), PF	500.00

LESOTHO	Unc.
1979 1 Sente, King Moshoeshoe II/hut (N-B)	.40
1992 2 Lisente, arms/bull (B)	.75
1966 50 Licente, King Moshoeshoe I/arms (S)	12.00
1988 10 Maloti, Pope/arms (S), PF	45.00

Lesotho 1966 50 Licente

LIBERIA	VF
1937 1/2 Cent, elephant/palm tree (B)	.25
	Unc.
1968 1 Cent, elephant/palm tree and ship (C)	.75
2000 5 Cents, arms/dragon (AL)	1.00
	VF
1960 10 Cents, African Liberty/wreath (S)	1.00
1968 50 Cents, same (CN)	.60
1995 1 Dollar, captains James T. Kirk and Jean-Luc Picard/arms (CN)	7.50
1996 1 Dollar, arms/fish (CN)	30.00
1964 20 Dollars, William V.S. Tubman/arms (G)	485.00

Liberia 1996 Dollar

MALAWI	Unc.
1964 1 Shilling, President Banda/corn (CNZ)	2.50
1971 1 Tambala, same/rooster (C)	.75
1995 5 Kwacha, President Muluzi/child reading (CN)	8.50

MALI	Unc.
1961 5 Francs, hippopotamus head (AL)	2.00
1967 50 Francs, President Keita (G), PF	425.00

MOZAMBIQUE	Unc.
1975 5 Centimos, head r./plant (CZ)	110.00
1986 20 Meticais, arms/armored tank (AL)	3.00
1994 10 Meticais, arms/cotton plant (B-clad St.)	1.25

NAMIBIA	Unc.
1993 10 Cents, arms/tree (N-plated St.)	1.00
1996 10 Dollars, arms/runner and cheetah (S), PF	35.00

Mali 1961 5 Francs

NIGER	PF
1960 500 Francs, President Hamani/arms (S)	35.00
1968 50 Francs, lion/arms (G)	450.00

Niger 1960 500 Francs

NIGERIA	Unc.
1973 1/2 Kobo, arms (C)	3.50
1991 1 Kobo, arms/oil wells (C-plated St.)	.25
1993 1 Naira, arms/Herbert Macaulay (N-plated St.)	1.75

RWANDA	Unc.
1965 1 Franc, head/arms (CN)	1.75
1970 2 Francs, person pouring grain/arms (AL, scalloped)	.50
1987 5 Francs, plant/arms (C)	1.85
1990 2,000 Francs, Nelson Mandela/arms (G), PF	250.00

SIERRA LEONE	Unc.
1964 1/2 Cent, Milton Margai/two fish (C)	.25
1980 1/2 Cent, Siaka Stevens/arms (C)	1.00
1978 10 Cents, Siaka Stevens/arms (CN)	1.00
1987 1 Leone, Joseph Momoh/arms (B, octagonal)	1.50
1998 10 Dollars, arms/Princess Diana (S), PF	37.50

SOMALIA	Unc.
1967 5 Centesimi, arms (B)	.60
1976 10 Senti, arms/lamb (AL, polygonal)	.50
2000 10 Shillings, arms/snake (St.)	1.00
(1984) 25 Shillings, arms/turtle (CN)	35.00

Somalia 1976 10 Senti

Republic of South Africa 1990 Rand

REPUBLIC OF SOUTH AFRICA	Unc.
1963 1/2 Cent, Jan Van Riebeeck/two sparrows confronted (B)	2.00
1961 1 Cent, Jan Van Riebeeck/wagon (B)	1.50
1969 1 Cent, similar/two sparrows (C)	.50
1971 2 Cents, arms/gnu (C)	.50
1978 5 Cents, arms/crane (N)	.75
1984 10 Cents, arms/aloe (N)	.35
1988 20 Cents, arms/protea (N)	.60
1992 50 Cents, arms/plant (B-plated St.)	1.00
1971 1 Rand, arms/springbok (S)	6.50
1990 1 Rand, arms/springbok (S), PF	25.00
1994 1 Rand, arms/building (S), PF	22.50
1994 5 Rand, similar (N-plated C)	5.50

Above two for inauguration of Nelson Mandela.

| 1978 Krugerrand, Paul Kruger/springbok (G, 1 ounce net) | BV + 3% |

SWAZILAND	Unc.
1974 1 Cent, King Sobhuza II/pineapple (C)	.20
1996 20 Cents, King Mswati III/elephant (CN, scalloped)	2.25
1996 50 Cents, King Mswati III/arms (CN)	3.75

TANZANIA	Unc.
1966 20 Senti, Julius Nyerere/ostrich (N-B)	1.50
1972 1 Shilingi, same/arms with torch (CN)	1.50
1992 20 Shilingi, Ali Hassan Mwinyi/mother and baby elephants (N-clad St.)	3.25
1974 1,500 Shilingi, Julius Nyerere/cheetah (G)	900.00
1998 2,500 Shilingi, arms/lions (S), PF	110.00

Tanzania 1998 2,500 Shilingi

UGANDA	Unc.
1966 10 Cents, tusks (C)	.35
1966 2 Shillings, arms/crowned crane (CN)	5.00
1987 10 Shillings, arms (St., heptagonal)	3.50
1993 10,000 Shillings, arms/Pope (S), PF	37.50

Uganda 1993 10,000 Shillings

WEST AFRICAN STATES	Unc.
1972 1 Franc, Ibex/root (AL)	.60
1980 25 Francs, chemist/root (ALB)	1.75
1982 5,000 Francs, root/seven shields (S)	45.00

West African States 1972 Franc

ZAMBIA	Unc.
1964 6 Pence, shield/morning glory (CNZ)	1.20
1968 1 Ngwee, Kenneth Kaunda/aardvark (C)	1.50
1972 50 Ngwee, same/arms (CN, polygonal)	4.50
1992 5 Kwacha, arms/oryx (B)	2.00
1998 100 Kwacha, arms/antelopes (S), PF	55.00

ZIMBABWE	Unc.
1980 1 Cent, ancient bird sculpture (C)	.40
1980 50 Cents, same/sunrise (CN)	2.25
1996 10 Dollars, Victoria Falls Bridge/lions (S), PF	55.00

Zambia 1998 100 Kwacha

ASIAN, NORTH AFRICAN & PACIFIC COINS

Most early Asian coins fit neatly into either the Islamic or Oriental category. Some pieces, particularly those of Southern India and Southeast Asia, have a distinctive appearance reflecting neither of these influences. Over the course of the 1800s, however, nearly all coinage based on these traditions—be they Islamic, Oriental, or local—were replaced by machine-made, European-style coinage. The images on these new, modern coins varied from an attempt to preserve traditional designs with modern forms to overt imitation of European motifs.

Trends in Islamic coinage changed following the fall of the Ottoman Empire after World War I. Today, few countries follow the strict Muslim prohibition of depicting persons or animals on coins. The traditional tughra symbol rarely appears these days, and Turkey even abandoned the Arabic alphabet for the Roman one. Also, a great number of Islamic countries produce bilingual coins. English or French often appears on the coins in a secondary position to Arabic. This is almost always the case with commemorative coins, which are largely produced for the international collector market.

It is ironic that the militant Taliban government of Afghanistan struck collector-market commemoratives depicting ancient pagan deities while it was planning to destroy the ancient statues of deities. Also, Western A.D. calendar dates often supplement the Islamic A.H. date; the former is used in some Islamic countries for business purposes.

In the center of the Middle East is its one non-Muslim country, Israel. It was founded in 1948 as a safe haven for Jews persecuted during World War II who sought to return to their ancient homeland. It is the only nation whose coins are inscribed in Hebrew, although Arabic and English are found on many issues as well. Israeli minor coins frequently have motifs from ancient Judean coinage. The extensive series of commemoratives features diverse motifs, often rendered in modern styles of art. During the 1960s and 1970s, Israeli commemorative coins were so widely purchased by the collecting public that now the number of coins and mint sets available from that time greatly exceeds demand, resulting in low prices. This was further complicated by the use of government-issued holders composed of a plastic corrosive to the coins' surfaces. Lower mintages and distribution, especially during the 1990s, have resulted in collector issues of somewhat more stable value.

Those looking for coinage struck by India before the colonial era will find listings for a sampling of numerous small states with unfamiliar names. This is because until 1947, India was not one unified country but a group of hundreds of princely states. Even during the period of British rule, only about half the country was directly controlled by the crown. Princely states—from the size of a city to those larger than most modern countries—often struck their own coins.

The first ancient Indian coins were not struck with a pair of dies, as were Western coins, or cast in molds, as were Chinese coins. Instead, they were impressed by several different punches on each side indicating sequence or authority. After the invasion of Alexander the Great, Western methods gradually took over. For a few hundred years after, most Indian coins were stylistic descendants of either Greek or Sassanian (Persian) coins. After the advent of Islam in the 8th century, most of central and northern India, regardless of the population's religion, used the Islamic-style coins discussed above. The largest states during this period were the Sultanate of Delhi and later the Mogul Empire. While all this occurred, southern India followed a different course. Most of the coins of this region freely bore images, generally of Hindu deities or their symbols. Gold, silver and copper were common in the north and south during most periods. Interestingly, however, Indian gold included tiny pieces called fanams. Struck in great quantities by princes and merchants, they were common from the 1600s to the 1800s, but some are from much earlier.

By the 1700s, most Indian coins were thick and were struck with dies larger than their blanks, thus only part of the design was impressed. The nickname for this style coin is "dump" coinage. Sometimes broad, ceremonial versions of the same coins were struck. These are called nazarana coins and are scarce for all but a few states. As time progressed, thinner, European-style coins began to replace dump coinage. Also from the 1700s to the present, designs consisting solely of inscriptions gradually gave way to images. In the case of one of the largest of the Muslim-ruled states, Hyderabad, the prohibition of living things on coins resulted in beautiful architectural depictions or a tughra similar to that of the Ottoman Empire.

It is interesting to note that Indian states coins are presently so poorly published and sparsely collected that uncataloged dates and varieties of many coins will occasionally sell for only a few dollars over the price a common one would fetch. Many of the silver and gold coins from this period bear small digs, called "shroff" marks, applied by bankers. If the marks are moderate, they only moderately reduce a coin's value in average condition.

After independence from Britain was achieved, the Indian subcontinent was divided into Bangladesh, the Republic of India, and Pakistan, with Ceylon, now Sri Lanka, off the coast. India's coinage, with massive mintages, is among the most common in the world. Its designs almost always feature the Asoka Pillar, a third century B.C. sculpture featuring lions facing in four directions. Recent Pakistani coins have omitted English legends but are characterized by the star and crescent motif. Both Bangladesh and India have used their coins extensively to promote increased agricultural production.

Until recently, Himalayan countries rarely placed portraits on their coins. Like non-Islamic India, they used religious symbols. Tibetan coins show some temporary Chinese influence in the 1800s. Other Central Asian countries during the medieval through early modern ages are properly discussed under Islamic coins. They then fell under Russian domination, first czarist then communist. Only Mongolia and Tuva maintained modern coinage during this period; Tuva's coinage is quite scarce. After the fall of the Soviet Union, many of these areas resumed coinage, combining European-style design with traditional artistic motifs.

Late in the 1800s, domestically made silver coins became common in China. These pieces, struck with European-style machinery by the imperial government, generally depicted a dragon, a motif picked up by Japan and Korea as well. As the Western-style silver became common, Western-style copper coins, generally without a central hole, began to replace the old cast cash coins. All three monarchies frequently dated their coins by the regal year of their emperors. China also used the traditional Oriental cyclical calendar. When the republic replaced the empire, portraits of politicians replaced the imperial dragon on silver, and flags replaced it on copper. Architecture also became a common theme beginning in the 1940s in China and Japan. Today, portraiture is not overwhelmingly favored in the Far East, but plants and animals have become popular, especially when they are symbolically significant.

In addition to China, many other areas of Asia progressed through a stage of primitive implement money. What is unusual about some of this is that it occasionally followed the initial introduction of coinage proper and continued in use concurrently with it. This is particularly true of Southeast Asia. Most of the coinage of Vietnam over the last several hundred years has been cast copper, although silver was slightly more common than in China. As European-style coinage was adopted in Southeast Asia, portraiture became common. Those depicted were usually kings in the case of Thailand and Cambodia, politicians in the case of Vietnam. This trend continued in the postwar era in many countries, although buildings, flora and fauna became common, too, particularly with the independence of Indonesia, Malaysia and Singapore. None of these countries has issued precious-metal coinage for circulation since 1942.

Independent Pacific coinage is a relatively recent phenomenon. Many nations did not even begin coinage until the 1970s. All the circulating coins are base metal, and a large percentage of the coins in both base and precious metals are struck for international collector distribution rather than circulation. Some countries, such as the Marshall Islands, have bolstered sales by making virtually false claims of legal-tender status. As a result, many are traded today at a fraction of their nominal face values or issue prices.

Known Counterfeits: Most portrait silver dollars of China have been extensively counterfeited. Those depicting Sun Yat-sen are often less deceptive than the others. Dragon dollars and Yuan Shih Kai dollars (called by many Chinese "fat man" dollars) have been counterfeited by the thousands. Many have a gray cast or are of incorrect weight. Counterfeits of dragon coppers made originally to circulate are often worth more than the real thing. In addition, there are now many fantasy "silver dollars" made of base metal, apparently originating in the same factories. Some feature new designs in the 1875-1930s style. Others are combinations of accurately engraved obverses and reverses that were never originally combined. Be careful not to take these as real rarities. If a coin is not in any of the books, it is probably fake rather than an unlisted authentic piece.

The Japanese 1,000 yen for the 1964 Olympics has been counterfeited. The details of the mountain differ. A number of experts have challenged the Japanese government's claims that counterfeits exist of the gold 100,000 yen.

Afghanistan 1999 500 Afghanis

AFGHANISTAN 1978-92	BU
1978 AD 500 Afghani, state seal/Siberian crane (S)	600.00

Islamic State, 1992-2001	BU
1999 50 Afghanis, state seal/Athena and equestrian (CN)	8.00
1999 500 Afghanis, arms/globe (S), PF	30.00

The Taliban Islamic State struck no coins for circulation, just for the collector market.

AJMAN (member of UAE)	Unc.
1969 1 Riyal, flags and bird (S)	8.00
1970 7-1/2 Riyals, emir/falcon (S)	55.00

Ajman 1969 Riyal

ALGERIA	Unc.
1964 1 Centime, arms (AL)	1.00
1964 50 Centimes, arms (ALB)	2.00
1974 5 Centimes, "1974-1977" inside gear (AL)	.75
1992 2 Dinars, camel head (St.)	5.00
1979 10 Dinars, elaborate inscription (ALB)	8.00
1993 100 Dinars, horse head (St. around ALB)	20.00
BAHRAIN	**Unc.**
1965 1 Fils, palm tree (C)	.40
1992 50 Fils, sailboats (CN)	1.50
1992 100 Fils, arms (B around CN)	3.50
1968 500 Fils, bust of amir/arms (S)	12.50
2000 500 Fils, monument, STATE OF BAHRAIN (CN around B)	6.00
1998 5 Dinars, amir/children (S), PF	36.50

Bahrain 1998 5 Dinars

BANGLADESH	Unc.
1973 5 Poisha, state seal/hoe (AL, square)	.20
1975 Taka, state seal/family (CN)	1.00
1992 Taka, state seal/runners (S), PF	32.50

Bangladesh 1992 Taka

Bhutan 1997 50 Ngultrums

BHUTAN	VF
(1928) 1/2 Rupee, king/symbols innine compartments (S)	15.00
(1928-68) 1/2 Ruppe, same but (N)	3.00 Unc.
1975 5 Chetrums, king/wheel (AL, square)	.20
1974 20 Chetrums, farmer/four-fold ornament (ALB)	.50
1997 50 Ngultrums, dragons, mansion (S), PF	20.00
1995 300 Ngultrums, dragons/Dag Hammarskjold (S), PF	32.50

BURMA (presently Myanmar)	Unc.
1952 1 Pya, lion (C)	.35
1966 25 Pya, Gen. Aung San (AL)	1.25
1953 1 Kyat, lion (CN)	2.00
1975 1 Kyat, rice plant (CN)	2.00

CAMBODIA	Unc.
1959 10 Sen, bird (AL)	1.00
1970 1 Riel, Angkor Wat (CN)	16.50
1974 10,000 Riels, bust of Lon Nol (S)	110.00
1979 5 Sen, arms (AL)	3.00
1993 4 Riels, flag/dinosaur (CN)	25.00
1994 100 Riels, Angkor Wat (St.)	.50

Cambodia 1959 10 Sen

CHINA, EMPIRE

Anhwei Province	VF
1902-1906 10 Cash, dragon (C)	6.00
1 struck cash, four characters/two characters (B, round hole)	2.00
Fukien 1896-1903 20 Cents, dragon (S)	7.00
Kiangsi c. 1902 10 Cash, dragon (C)	2.00
Kwangtung 1890-1908 10 Cents, dragon (S)	4.50
Pei Yang (Chihli) 1908 Dollar, dragon, 34th year (S)	125.00
Szechuan Province	VF
1906 10 Cash, dragon (C)	3.00
(1901-08) Dollar, dragon (S)	30.00
CHINA, REPUBLIC (General Issues)	VF
1916 1/2 Cent, diamond with border of buds (C, holed)	10.00
1936 1/2 Cent, sun/ancient spade money (C)	1.50
C. 1920 10 Cash	1.50
(1912-27) 10 Cash, crossed flags (C)	1.50
1940 1 Cent, sun/ancient spade money (B)	.75
1940 1 Cent, ancient spade money (AL)	.25
(1912-27) 20 Cash, crossed flags (C)	2.50
1933 2 Cents, diamond with border of buds (C, holed)	60.00
1936 5 Cents, Sun Yat-sen/ancient spade money (N)	1.50
1940 5 Cents, ancient spade money (AL)	1.00
1914 1 Chiao, bust of Gen. Yuan Shi-kai (S)	10.00

CHINA, REPUBLIC (General Issues)	VF
1941 10 Cents, Sun Yat-sen/ancient spade money (CN)	1.50
1926 20 Cents, phoenix and dragon (S)	15.00
1927 20 Cents, Sun Yat-sen facing/crossed flags (S)	25.00
1914 50 Cents, Yuan Shi-kai/wreath (S)	45.00
1942 50 Cents, Sun Yat-sen/ancient spade money (CN)	3.00
1914 Dollar, Yuan Shi-kai/wreath (S)	300.00
C. 1918 Dollar, Yuan Shi-kai in high hat/dragon (S)	300.00
(1912-27) Dollar, Sun Yat-sen/MEMENTO over wreath (S)	300.00
1932 Dollar, Sun Yat-sen/junk sailing into sunrise, birds over head (S)	300.00
1934 Dollar, similar but no birds or sun (S)	17.00
1916 10 Dollars, Hung-hsien/dragon (G)	2,500.00

China, Republic-General Issues 1920 10 Cash

CHINA, REPUBLIC (Province Issues)	VF
Anwhei 1902-1906 10 Cash, rosette in center/English legend above dragon (C)	6.00
Chekiang 1924 10 Cents, crossed flags (S)	7.00
Fengtien 1929 1 Cent, sun over wreath (C)	3.00
Fukien 1923 20 Cents, three flags (S)	7.50
Honan (1912-27) 10 Cash, crossed flags (C)	2.00
Hunan (1912-27) 10 Cash, star (C)	4.00
Kansu 1928 Dollar, Sun Yat-sen/star (S)	1,800.00
Kiangsi 1912 10 Cash, star (C)	5.00
Kwangsi-Kwangsea 1926 20 Cents, "20" (S)	6.50
Kwangtung 1914 1 Cent, value (C)	5.00
Kwangtung 1919 20 Cents, "20" (S)	3.50
Kweichow 1928 Dollar, auto (S)	2,000.00
Shensi (1928) 2 Cents, crossed flags and IMTYPEF (C)	40.00
Singkiang 1949 Dollar, value (S)	35.00
Szechuan 1906 10 Cash, Chinese characters only on each side (C)	3.00
Szechuan 1912 Dollar, seal script (S)	22.00

China, Empire-Province Issues Anhwei 1902-1906 10 Cash

China, Republic-Province Issues Kwangtung 1914 Cent

China, Empire-Province Issues Szechuan 1906 10 Cash

CHINA, REPUBLIC OF TAIWAN	Unc.
1949 1 Chiao, Sun Yat-sen/map of Taiwan (C)	4.00
1954 5 Chiao, similar (B)	1.00
1960 1 Yuan, flowers (CNZ)	.50
1970 5 Yuan, Chaing Kai-shek l. (CN)	1.50
1981 5 Yuan, same (CN)	.50
1989 10 Yuan, Chaing Kai-shek facing (CN)	.75
2000 10 Yuan, dragon/stylized dragon (CN)	3.00
1965 100 Yuan, Sun Yat-sen/deer (S)	27.50

China, Republic of Taiwan 1981 5 Yuan

CHINA, PEOPLE'S REPUBLIC	Unc.
1976 1 Fen, arms (AL)	.50
1956 2 Fen, arms (AL)	1.50
1986 5 Fen, arms (AL)	.45
1992 1 Jiao, arms/flower (AL)	.50
1980 1 Yuan, Great Wall (CN)	2.00
1991 Yuan, soccer balls/female goalie (St.)	2.50
1986 5 Yuan, Great Wall/ship (S)	35.00 BU
1995 5 Yuan, monkey (C)	12.00
1995 10 Yuan, building/two pigs (S, scalloped), PF	110.00
1996 20 Yuan, city gate/Yangtze River (S, rectangular), PF	65.00
1989 100 Yuan, arms/snake (platinum), PF	2,400.00
1991 10,000 Yuan, Temple of Heaven/panda encircled by coins (G), PF	120,000.00

China, People's Republic 1991 Yuan

China, People's Republic 1996 20 Yuan

EGYPT, BRITISH OCCUPATION ISSUES	VF
1917 1/2 Millieme, inscription (C)	5.00
1916 5 Milliemes, inscription (CN, hole)	5.00
1917 2 Piastres, inscription (S)	4.50
1916 100 Piastres, inscription (G)	220.00
Fuad I, 1917-36	**VF**
1935 1 Millieme, King Fuad (C)	.50
1935 5 Milliemes, King Fuad (CN)	1.00
1923 10 Piastres, King Fuad (S)	22.50
1930 50 Piastres, King Fuad (G)	115.00
Farouk I, 1936-52	**VF**
1938 1 Millieme (C)	.50
1938 5 Milliemes, King Farouk (C, scalloped)	1.00
1938 10 Milliemes, King Farouk (C, scalloped edge)	1.00
1941 10 Milliemes, King Farouk (CN)	1.00
1944 2 Piastres, King Farouk (S, hexagonal)	1.50
1938 100 Piastres, King Farouk (G)	220.00

Egypt 1938 Millieme

Republic 1952-58	Unc.
1956 1 Millieme, sphinx (ALB)	5.00
1955 10 Piastres, sphinx (S)	18.00
1957 25 Piastres, building (S)	17.00
1958 1/2 Pound, ancient chariot (G)	200.00

United Arab Republic, 1958-71	Unc.
1962 2 Milliemes, falcon (ALB)	.65
1958 20 Milliemes, gear (ALB)	5.00
1960 5 Piastres, falcon (S)	5.00
1964 5 Piastres, dam (S)	4.00
1967 10 Piastres, falcon (CN)	2.00
1970 25 Piastres, nasser (S)	6.50
1970 1 Pound, mosque (S)	13.00
1960 5 Pounds, dam (G)	1,100.00

Arab Republic of Egypt	Unc.
1975 5 Milliemes, Nefertiti (B)	.30
1984 1 Piastre, Tughra/pyramids (ALB)	.35
1972 5 Piastres, falcon (CN)	2.00
1977 10 Piastres, clasped hands (CN)	3.00
1980 10 Piastres, Sadat (CN)	4.50

Arab Republic of Egypt	Unc.
1992 10 Piastres, mosque (B)	2.00
1973 1 Pound, dam (S)	15.00
1980 1 Pound, fist (S)	15.00
1994 5 Pounds, ancient hippopotamus figure (S), PF	45.00

Egypt 1992 10 Piastres

FUJAIRAH (member of UAE)	Unc.
1969 2 Riyals, Richard Nixon (S), PF	30.00
1969 10 Riyals, Apollo XI astronauts (S), PF	60.00
1970 25 Riyals, Richard Nixon (G), PF	165.00

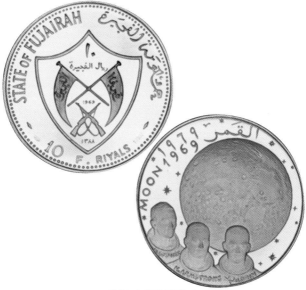

Fujairah 1969 10 Riyals

INDIAN STATES (presently parts of India, Pakistan, and Bangladesh)	F
Gwalior 1942 1/4 Anna, bust l. (C)	.75
Indore 1935 1/4 Anna, facing bust (C)	.50
Indore 1902 1/2 Anna, bull (C)	2.00
Jaipur 1944 1 Anna, bust/branch (B)	.25
Kutch 1928 5 Kori, inscriptions (S)	15.00
Mewar 1928 Rupee, city walls (S)	7.50
Pudokkatai 1889-1906 1 Cash, Goddess Brihadamba (C)	.75
Tonk 1932 Pice, arms/leaf (C)	.25

INDIA	F
1950 1 Pice, Asoka pillar/horse (C)	3.00
1954 1 Anna, similar/bull (CN, scalloped)	1.25
1950 1 Rupee, similar/two ears of grain (N)	4.50
1972 1 Paisa, Asoka pillar (AL, square)	.50
1961 2 Paise, similar (CN, scalloped)	.80
1970 3 Paise, similar (AL, hexagonal)	.50
1957 5 Paise, similar (CN, square)	1.00
1993 10 Paise, similar (St.)	.50
1968 20 Paise, similar/lotus (N-B)	1.50
1996 25 Paise, rhinoceros/Asoka pillar (St.)	1.00
1972 50 Paise, couple with flag/similar (CN)	1.00

INDIA	F
1991 1 Rupee, Rajiv Gandhi/similar (CN)	1.50
1997 1 Rupee, Asoka pillar/two ears of grain (St.)	.60
1994 2 Rupees, water drop/Asoka pillar (CN)	2.00
1997 2 Rupees, map/similar (CN)	1.00
(1985) "1984" 5 Rupees, Indira Gandhi/similar (CN)	3.00
1994 5 Rupees, denomination/similar (CN)	1.50
(1969-70) 10 Rupees, Mahatma Gandhi/similar (S)	9.00
1974 10 Rupees, family in triangle/similar (CN)	4.50
1986 20 Rupees, fishermen/similar (CN)	10.00
1975 50 Rupees, woman and ear of grain/similar (S)	11.50
1982 100 Rupees, Asian Games logo/similar (S)	17.50

India (Republic) 1997 Rupee

INDONESIA	Unc.
1952 1 Sen, rice (AL, hole)	.75
1970 1 Rupiah, bird (AL)	.50
1971 10 Rupiah, wreath (CN)	.50
1991 100 Rupiah, eagle/cow racing (ALB)	.60
1993 1,000 Rupiah, eagle/tree (CN around B)	3.50
1974 100,000 Rupiah, eagle/Komodo dragon (G)	875.00

IRAN (Pahlavi Dynasty, 1925-79)	XF
1971 100 Rials, ruins of Persepolis (S), PF	27.50

Indonesia 1952 Sen

IRAQ (Kingdom)	VF
1933 1 Fils, Faisal I (C)	3.00
1932 1 Riyal, Faisal I (S)	15.00
1938 4 Fils, Ghazi I (C)	1.00
1938 20 Fils, Ghazi I (S)	3.50
1953 100 Fils, Faisal II (S)	7.50
Republic	**Unc.**
1959 1 Fils, grain in star (C, polygonal)	1.00
1971 5 Fils, palm trees (St., scalloped)	.75
1970 100 Fils, similar (CN)	1.50
1973 1 Dinar, oil tanker (S)	20.00
1981 1 Dinar, Saddam Hussein and airplanes (N)	20.00
1971 5 Dinars, two soldiers (G)	370.00
ISRAEL	**Unc.**
1949 25 Mils, grapes (AL)	50.00
1949 1 Pruta, anchor (AL)	2.00
1949 5 Prutot, lyre (C)	2.50
1952 10 Prutot, ancient jug (AL, scalloped)	2.00
1954 100 Pruta, date palm (N-clad St.)	3.00
1949 500 Pruta, three pomegranates (S)	35.00
1965 1 Agora, three ears of grain (AL, scalloped)	.25
1979 1/2 Lira, menorah (CN)	.50
1967 10 Lirot, sword and olive branch/Western Wall (S)	11.50

Israel 1952 10 Prutot

Israel 1980 New Agora

ISRAEL	Unc.
1969 10 Lirot, helmet and inscription (S)	14.00
1974 25 Lirot, David Ben-Gurion/menorah (S)	14.50
1980 1 New Agora, date palm (AL)	.20
1982 1/2 Sheqel, lion (CN)	1.00
1984 1 Sheqel, Theresianstadt lamp (S)	17.00
1984 10 Sheqalim, ancient ship (CN)	1.25
1984 100 Sheqalim, ancient coin with menorah (CN)	1.50
1986 1 New Sheqel, lily (CN)	1.50
1988 1 New Sheqel, Maimonides (CN)	1.75
1996 1 New Sheqel, Yitzak Rabin (S)	35.00
1998 1 New Sheqel, Noah (S)	30.00
1991 10 New Sheqalim, jumbo jet and immigrants (G), PF	475.00
1995 10 New Sheqalim, date palm (aureate, bronze, N, St.)	5.00

Israel 1984 Sheqel

Israel 1984 10 Sheqalim

Israel 1995 10 New Sheqalim

JAPAN

Meiji	VF
1907 20 Sen, sunburst (S)	4.00
1905 50 Sen, dragon (S)	10.00
1903 1 Yen, dragon (S)	40.00
Taisho	VF
1916 5 Rin, paulowina crest (C)	1.50
1913 1 Sen, sunburst (C)	2.25
1917 10 Sen, sunburst (S)	1.50
1925 50 Sen, sunburst/two phoenix depictions (S)	1.75
Showa	Unc.
1941 1 Sen, Mount Fuji (AL)	.50
1938 10 Sen, cherry blossom/waves (ALB, hole)	4.75

Japan 1905 50 Sen

Showa	Unc.
1946 50 Sen, phoenix (B)	2.50
1968 5 Yen, rice plant (B)	.10
1978 50 Yen, chrysanthemums (CN, hole)	1.25
1958 100 Yen, phoenix (S)	5.00
1977 100 Yen, bridge/chrysanthemum (CN)	5.00
1964 1,000 Yen, Mount Fuji (S)	30.00
1986 100,000 Yen, chrysanthemum/two phoenix depictions (G)	1,000.00

Heisei	Unc.
1990 Yen, sapling (AL)	.10
1997 10 Yen, temple (C)	.40
1994 50 Yen, chrysanthemums (CN, hole)	.75
1989 500 Yen, paulowina (CN)	10.00
1993 5,000 Yen, chrysanthemum/two cranes (S)	60.00

Japan 1977 100 Yen

JORDAN	Unc.
1949 1 Fils, crown (C)	2.25
same but Fils misspelled "Fil"	3.50
1975 50 Fils, King Hussein (CN)	1.25
1977 2-1/2 Dinars, King Hussein/gazelle (S)	25.00
1995 1 Dinar, similar/FAO logo (B)	10.00
1981 60 Dinars, similar/Palace of Culture (G), PF	450.00
2000 5 Piastres, King Abdullah (N-clad St.)	2.00

Jordan 1977 2-1/2 Dinars

KAZAKHSTAN	Unc.
1993 2 Tyin, arms (B)	.45
1995 20 Tenge, arms/U.N. logo (CN)	3.50
1996 20 Tenge, arms/musician (CN)	3.50
2000 50 Tenge, arms/mosque (CN)	3.00
1995 100 Tenge, arms/old man and hut (S), PF	35.00

Kazakhstan 2000 50 Tenge

KIRIBATI	Unc.
1979 5 Cents, arms/Tokai lizard (CN)	1.50
1979 1 Dollar, arms/outrigger sailboat (CN)	4.00
1997 5 Dollars, arms/castle (S), PF	40.00

KOREA	VF
1910 10 Chon, dragon (S)	35.00

NORTH KOREA	Unc.
1959 1 Chon, arms (AL)	1.00
1987 1 Won, building/arms (AL)	4.00
1995 10 Won, arms/cartoon cat (CN)	10.00
1997 10 Won, flower/arms (S)	55.00

SOUTH KOREA	Unc.
1959 100 Hwan, Syngman Rhee/two phoenix depictions (CN)	10.00
1978 1 Won, Rose of Sharon (AL)	.15
1973 50 Won, rice plant (CN)	3.50
1983 50 Won, similar	.45
1983 500 Won, Manchurian crane (CN)	2.50
1984 10,000 Won, cross/saints (S)	20.00
1998 10,000 Won, logo (S)	35.00

North Korea 1997 10 Won

South Korea 1998 10,000 Won

KUWAIT	BU
1976 1 Fils, ship (N-B)	.75
1962 50 Fils, ship (CN)	1.50
1976 2 Dinars, two busts/oil well and ship (S)	50.00

Kuwait 1976 2 Dinars

LAOS	Unc.
1952 20 Cents, elephants (AL)	2.00
1971 2,500 Kip, king/arms (S)	35.00
1980 20 Att, arms/plower (AL)	.85
1995 50 Kip, dinosaur (S), PF	25.00

Laos 1971 2,500 Kip

LEBANON	VF
1925 1 Piastre, wreath/lion heads (CN, hole)	2.00
1925 2 Piastres, cedar/Phoenician ship (B)	8.00
1929 25 Piastres, cedar/two cornucopias (S)	7.00
1955 1 Piastre, wreath (ALB, hole)	1.50
1975 10 Piastres, cedar (N-B)	.20
1952 50 Piastres, cedar (S)	4.50
1968 1 Livre, cedar/fruit (N)	3.50
1980 400 Livres, monogram/olympic logo (G), PF	600.00

Lebanon 1929 25 Piastres

LIBYA	Unc.
1952 1 Millieme, King Idris (C)	.75
1952 5 Milliemes, King Idris (C)	1.50
1965 10 Milliemes, crowned arms (CN)	.50
1975 10 Dirhams, eagle (CN-clad St.)	2.25
1979 100 Dirhams, horseman with rifle (CN)	9.00
1981 70 Dinars, hands embracing handicap symbol/logo (G)	475.00

MALAYSIA	Unc.
1967 1 Sen, building (C)	2.00
1989 5 Sen, top (CN)	.20
1993 1 Ringgit, dagger and scabbard (B)	1.75
1976 500 Ringgit, Malayan tapir (G)	950.00

MARSHALL ISLANDS	Unc.
1986 1 Dollar, arms/triton shell (S), PF	25.00
1988 5 Dollars, arms/space shuttle Discovery (CN)	4.50
1989 5 Dollars, arms/man on moon (CN)	3.50
1993 10 Dollars, arms/Elvis Presley (B)	16.50
1993 50 Dollars, arms/dolphins (S)	60.00
1995 50 Dollars, arms/Marilyn Monroe (S), PF	56.00

Marshall Islands 1993 50 Dollars

MONGOLIA	XF
1925 1 Tugrik, national emblem (S)	22.00
1937 20 Mongo, similar (CN)	10.00
1937 5 Mongo, similar (ALB)	6.00
1945 5 Mongo, arms (ALB)	5.00
1959 2 Mongo, wreath (AL, hole)	1.50
1981 1 Mongo, arms (AL)	.85
1992 250,000 Tugrik, Ghengis Khan/national emblem (G), PF	28,500.00

Mongolia 1959 2 Mongo

MOROCCO	VF
1951 1 Franc, star (AL)	.25
1953 100 Francs, star within star (S)	2.00
	Unc.
1975 5 Santimat, arms/wheel and fish (B)	1.00
1965 1 Dirham, Hasan II/arms (N)	2.00
1987 5 Dirham, similar (St. around ALB)	7.50
1986 100 Dirhams, pope and king/arms (S)	100.00
MYANMAR	**Unc.**
1999 5 Kyats, lion (B)	.50
1999 50 Kyats, lion (CN)	1.75
NEJD (presently part of Saudi Arabia)	**VF**
C. 1917, "Nejd" countermarked in Arabic on Egypt 5 Piastres (S) These have been counterfeited.	100.00
NEPAL	**VF**
1902 1 Paisa, inscription in square (C)	4.00
1953 5 Paisa, urn (CN)	2.00
1932 1 Rupee, trident/sword (S)	10.00
1934 1 Rupee, similar but neater (S)	6.00
	Unc.
1980 5 Paisa, mountain/cow (AL)	.75
1993 25 Paisa, crown (AL)	.50
1971 50 Paisa, trident/sword (CN)	.50
1968 10 Rupee, king with plumed helmet (S)	9.00
1993 500 Rupee, bear (S), PF	45.00

NIUE	Unc.
1997 1 Dollar, arms/Princess Diana (CN)	4.50
1997 5 Dollars, arms/Queen Mother (S), PF	18.00
1997 10 Dollars, arms/Princess Diana (S), PF	15.00
1992 5 Dollars, arms/HMS Bounty (S)	9.00

Niue 1997 5 Dollars

Niue 1997 10 Dollars

Oman 1975 5 Baisa

OMAN (formerly Muscat and Oman)	Unc.
1975 5 Baisa, dagger and swords (C)	.45
1980 1/4 Rial, same (ALB)	2.00
1994 1/2 Rial, sultan/dagger and swords (S), PF	110.00

PALESTINE MANDATE	VF
1927 1 Mil, branch (C)	2.00
1927 20 Mils, wreath (CN, hole)	12.00
1942 50 Mils, branch (S)	8.00

PAKISTAN	Unc.
1951 1 Pie, tughra (C)	2.50
1948 2 Annas, tughra/star and crescent (CN)	1.00
1961 1 Pice, tower, star and crescent (AL)	.30
1962 5 Paisa, tughra, star and crescent/ship (N-B)	1.00
1976 50 Paisa, Mohammed Ali Jinnah (CN)	1.50
1998 2 Rupees, mosque (N-B)	.85
1976 150 Rupees, tower, star and crescent/crocodile (S)	40.00

Pakistan 1976 150 Rupees

PHILIPPINES	Unc.
1958 1 Centavo, arms/man seated with hammer (C)	.25
1964 25 Centavos, arms/woman with hammer (CNZ)	.35
1947 50 Centavos, MacArthur/arms (S)	7.50
1967 1 Peso, flaming sword/arms (S)	7.00
1974 1 Sentimo, Lapulapu (AL)	.10
1983 50 Sentimos, pilar/eagle (CN)	1.25
1970 1 Piso, Marcos/Pope Paul VI (N)	2.25
1990 2 Piso, Bonifacio/tree (CN)	1.25
1974 25 Piso, arms/national bank (S)	7.00
1979 50 Piso, child (S)	9.00
1992 10,000 Pesos, Corazon Aqino/map (G), PF	950.00

Philippines 1974 25 Piso

Qatar 1973 50 Dirhems

QATAR	Unc.
1973 1 Dirhem, ship and trees (C)	1.00
1973 50 Dirhems, similar (CN)	2.00
(1998) 500 Riyals, similar/bank building (G), PF	700.00
QATAR & DUBAI	**Unc.**
1966 1 Dirhem, gazelle (C)	8.00
RAS AL KHAIMAH (member of UAE)	**Unc.**
1970 50 Dirhams, falcon (CN)	45.00
1970 2-1/2 Rials, Emir/falcon (S)	75.00
1970 10 Riyals, Eisenhower (S)	18.50
SAUDI ARABIA	**Unc.**
1978 100 Halala (CN)	3.50
SHARJAH	**Unc.**
1964 5 Rupees, John F. Kennedy/crossed flags (S)	15.00

Saudi Arabia 1978 100 Halala

Singapore 1978 10 Dollars

SINGAPORE	Unc.
1986 1 Cent, arms (C)	.10
1971 5 Cents, fish (AL)	1.00
1967 20 Cents, swordfish (CN)	.75
1974 50 Cents, zebra fish (CN)	2.00
1978 10 Dollars, satellite dish (S)	12.50
1981 5 Dollars, airport (CN)	10.00
1990 100 Dollars, arms/lion head (G)	1,000.00
SOUTH ARABIA	Unc.
1964 1 Fils, daggers (AL)	.15
1964 50 Fils, boat (CN)	1.25
SRI LANKA (CEYLON)	Unc.
1963 1 Cent, arms (AL)	.10
1975 25 Cents, arms (CN)	.25
1981 2 Rupees, dam (CN)	2.50
1995 5 Rupees, U.N. logo (ALB)	2.50

Sudan 1975 10 Ghirsh

SUDAN	Unc.
1956 1 Millim, oostman on camel (C)	.30
1970 10 Millim, similar (C, scalloped)	1.00
1975 10 Ghirsh, arms (CN)	2.50
1989 25 Ghirsh, building (St.)	2.25
1976 5 Pounds, hippopotami (S)	25.00

SYRIA	VF
1919 Dinar, arms/wreath (G)	8,000.00
1935 1 Piastre, lion heads (B, hole)	2.50
1926 5 Piastres, crossed grain (B)	2.00
1929 10 Piastres, ornamental design (S)	12.00
ND (World War II emergency issue) 1 Piastre, inscription (B)	5.00

	Unc.
1971 5 Piastres, arms/grain (ALB)	.25
1950 1 Lira, arms (S)	25.00
1978 1 Pound, Assad/arms (N)	5.00
1995 25 Pounds, same (ALB around St.)	7.00
2003 25 Pounds, parliament (N-B around CN)	3.75
1997 10 Pounds, arms/map and flag, Baath Party 50th anniversary (CN)	2.50

Syria 1950 Lira

Syria 1971 5 Piastres

TANNU TUVA (presently part of Russia)	VF
1934 1 Kopejek (ALB)	50.00
1934 20 Kopejek (CN)	65.00

THAILAND	VF
1908 1 Baht, Rama V l./elephants (S)	2,500.00
1918 1 Baht, Rama VI r./elephants (S)	12.50
1929 50 Satang, Rama VII l./elephant l. (S)	7.00
1946 25 Satang, Rama VIII as child/Garuda (tin)	2.50

Rama IX	Unc.
1957 5 Satang, bust/arms (B)	2.00
1961 1 Baht, king and queen/arms (CN)	2.00
1972 5 Baht, bust/Garuda (CN, polygonal)	1.20
1980 10 Baht, bust/wheel (N)	2.50
1996 20 Baht, king with camera/king and people (CN)	3.50
1971 50 Baht, bust/wheel (S)	14.00

TIBET	VF
1919 1 Sho, lion (C)	5.00
1937 3 Srang, lion before mountains (S)	9.00
1952 10 Srang, similar (S)	15.00
1918 20 Srang, lion (G)	575.00
1902-42 Rupee, Chinese bust/floral wreath (S) struck by Chinese	35.00

TONGA	Unc.
1967 1 Seniti, Queen Salote (C)	1.00
1981 20 Seneti, King Taufa'ahau/roots (CN)	1.50
1985 1 Pa'anga, king/dove (CN, heptagonal)	2.75
1981 5 Hau, king/Charles and Diana (G)	450.00
1996 1 Pa'anga, arms/Elizabeth II (S), PF	22.50

Tonga 1996 Pa'anga

TUNISIA	Unc.
1954 5 Francs, monogram/crescent (CN)	5.00
1960 2 Millim, tree (AL)	.25
1976 1/2 Dinar, Bourguiba/hands (CN)	6.50
1969 1 Dinar, Bourguiba/Hannibal (S), PF	16.50
1982 75 Dinars, same/children (G), PF	450.00

TURKEY	VF
1928 25 Kurus, similar, Arabic alphabet (N)	3.00
1936 1 Kurus, star in crescent (CN)	5.00
1948 1 Lira, star and crescent (S)	3.00

	Unc.
1979 1 Kurus, girl in veil/branch (C)	3.00
1975 5 Kurus, similar/oak branch (C)	3.00
1967 1 Lira, Ataturk (St.)	10.00
1979 5 Lira, Ataturk on horse (St.)	1.00
1960 10 Lira, Ataturk/symbols of revolution (S)	10.00
1988 50 Lira, Ataturk (ALB)	.15
1997 5,000 Lira, Ataturk (B)	.75
1992 500,000 Lira, ship (Turkish Jews) (G), PF	320.00
1998 500,000 Lira, wreath/Ataturk (CN)	15.00
2000 150,000,000 Lira, mint logo/President Clinton (G in S), PF	750.00

Turkey 1979 Kurus

United Arab Emirates 1990 50 Dirhams

TURKMENISTAN	Unc.
1993 1 Tenge, Nyyazow (C-plated St.)	.25
1993 50 Tenge, same/rhyton (N-plated St.)	2.75

UNITED ARAB EMIRATES	Unc.
1973 1 Fils, palm trees (C)	.45
1973 50 Fils, oil wells (CN)	1.50
1995 1 Dirham, pitcher (CN)	1.85
1981 5 Dirhams, falcon (CN)	15.00
1990 50 Dirhams, bust of Sheikh/Dubai International Trade Center (S), PF	70.00

UZBEKISTAN	Unc.
1994 3 Tiyin, arms (B-clad St.)	1.00
1997 10 Som, arms (N-clad St.)	2.00

VIETNAM	Unc.
1976 1 Hao, arms (AL)	10.00
1987 10 Dong, arms/orangutan (CN)	20.00
1989 20 Dong, Ho Chi Minh (B), PF	14.50
1992 100 Dong, soccer (S), PF	25.00

Vietnam 1992 100 Dong

NORTH VIETNAM	XF
1946 5 Hao, stove/star (AL)	20.00
1958 1 Xu, wreath (AL, hole)	5.00
SOUTH VIETNAM	BU
1953 10 Su, three women (AL)	4.00
1960 1 Dong, bust/rice (AL)	2.50
1966 5 Dong, rice (CN, scalloped)	2.00
1974 10 Dong, farmers (B-clad St.)	2.00
1975 50 Dong, rice farmers (N-clad St.)	650.00

South Vietnam 1960 Dong

WESTERN SAMOA	Unc.
1967 1 Sene, king (C)	.30
1974 50 Sene, king/bananas (CN)	2.00
1974 1 Tala, boxers/arms (CN)	3.50
1988 100 Tala, arms/Kon-Tiki (G), PF	225.00
YEMEN ARAB REPUBLIC	Unc.
1963 1 Buqsha, leaves (ALB)	1.00
1979 25 Fils, arms (CN)	2.00
1974 50 Fils, arms (CN)	2.50
1963 1 Riyal, leaves (S)	13.50
1975 100 Riyals, eagle/"Arab Jerusalem" (G)	400.00
People's Democratic Republic	Unc.
1981 100 Fils, building (CN, octagonal)	3.00
Republic	Unc.
1995 10 Riyals, stone bridge (St.)	2.75

Yemen Arab Republic 1963 Riyal

Yemen 1974 50 Fils

COINS OF THE AMERICAS

The images and symbolism that adorned the newly independent Latin American countries' coins in the early 1800s found their origins in the coinages of the early United States and the French Revolution. This was only natural. After all, most of these states had rejected monarchy in favor of a representative republican form of government, quite unusual at the time. There were few examples of republican coinages on which to base their coins. The United States' was the closest, and its struggle showed that a colony can throw off its master's yoke. The French Republic had been the most important in terms of the development of political thought.

Hence, the first generations of Latin American coins were mostly dominated by female personifications of liberty as well as symbols of liberty and prosperity, such as the liberty cap and the cornucopia. This was not to the exclusion of real human portraiture. Haïti (the hemisphere's second oldest independent nation), Mexico and Brazil all established monarchies. These and many other countries depicted their heads of state, be it king or president or the liberator Simon Bolivar. Almost all of the new countries proudly displayed their new, distinctly American coats of arms.

If the primary inspiration for images was the United States and France, the primary source for the physical form and standard of the coinage was clearly Spain, the colonizing power for most of the New World. Most countries retained a silver coin the size of the old Spanish milled dollar, or 8-real piece. Some even kept its division into pieces of eight. Many gold pieces were also struck on the old escudo standard as well. Many of the big bullion exporting areas during colonial days continued to do so after independence, and the Mexican 8-real peso was a favorite coin in the Orient until the early 1900s.

Latin American coinage proved to be far less stable than the old Spanish colonial coinage. Within a generation or two, many of these new 8 reales, or pesos, declined in weight or purity. Some were even replaced by copper emergency coins. By 1967, all Latin American and Caribbean countries had abandoned precious metal for all but bullion and commemorative coins.

Iconography remained fairly consistent throughout the 1800s. Some of the biggest changes in the imagery reflected the overthrow of the Haitian (1806, 1821, 1858), Mexican (1823, 1867), and Brazilian (1889) monarchies. The diverse and creative allegories of Bolivian proclamation coins often incorporated books, buildings, crowds, and dragons as well as images of the presidents, who seemed to take power and be forced out with the vagaries of fate.

Another change was the replacement of the screw press with steam-powered machinery for the manufacture of coinage, generally within the first 50 years of independence. As a transition to modern minting technology, many Latin American countries toward the end of the century contracted to have their coins struck in Paris, Brussels, Birmingham (England), or Waterbury (Connecticut). Improvements in local die engraving were spotty, however, and images usually varied from quaint to cartoonlike. European mints provided not only high-capacity machines capable of producing uniform coins but expert die engraving as well.

New images appeared toward the beginning of the 20th century along with new metals. Commemoratives were also introduced, the first in Colombia in 1892 to honor the 400th anniversary of Columbus' discovery of America. During the period before the 1950s, Brazil and Mexico were the only other countries to release commemorative coins. Late in the 20th century, most New World countries struck commemoratives for circulation and sale to collectors at a premium. The flora and fauna depicted on many Caribbean and Central American coins have given them particular appeal to collectors.

Many New World collector issues have been distributed in Europe and North America by marketing firms. Excessive distribution, particularly in the case of Caribbean collector issues, caused sharp drops in their market prices, and many today can be purchased well below their original issue prices. Unknowingly, some collectors have further reduced the value of their holdings by discarding the original mint holders in which collector coins must remain to maintain their maximum value.

Plantation, or hacienda, tokens are one of the most fascinating aspects of Latin American numismatics. Some plantations were so large that they constituted company-run towns with exclusive, company-run stores. This was also true of some mines. Often the workers were paid with tokens issued by the plantation or mines that were good at these stores. They were usually simple, devoid of all but inscriptions and numbers, but form a valuable record of local history.

Known Counterfeits: Contemporary counterfeits of the early coppers of Brazil are quite common and actively collected. Cast counterfeits exist of the Cuban 1915 10, 20 and 40 centavos and peso, and 1932 peso. A counterfeit of the 1928 Ecuador 1 condor was struck with cast dies. Early Haitian silver coins were counterfeited at the time, but the counterfeits are collected along with the official issues. Contemporary counterfeits of Mexican cap-and-rays 8 reales abound. Most are struck in either nickel-silver (an alloy of copper, nickel and zinc but no silver) or a baser silver alloy. A partial list includes the 1835PiJS, 1836ZsOM, 1840GJ, 1843MoML, 1894MoAM, and 1904ZsFM (peso). Counterfeits of 2 and 4 reales of this type also exist. There are collector counterfeits of several of the Mexican revolutionary issues and dangerous counterfeits of some of the Mexican 20th-century bullion gold coins, the 1947 50 peso in particular. A 1982 counterfeit Mexico silver onza is not dangerous because of its significant difference in style. Another bullion piece, the Peru 1962 100 soles, has been the victim of a dangerous counterfeit of about 75-percent gold.

Argentina 1991 1,000 Australes

ARGENTINA (REPUBLIC)	VF
1903 5 Centavos, similar (CN)	.50
1915 10 Centavos, similar (CN)	1.00
1926 20 Centavos, similar (CN)	.50
1941 50 Centavos, similar (N)	1.00
1959 1 Peso, similar (N-clad St.)	1.50
	Unc.
1963 5 Pesos, sailing ship (N-clad St.)	2.00
1963 10 Pesos, gaucho (N-clad St.)	2.00
1973 1 Centavo, head of Argentina/olive branch (AL)	.30
1986 5 Centavos, wildcat (B)	1.50
2000 50 Centavos, guemes/value (B)	2.50
1991 1,000 Australes, 14 coats of arms/globes and pillars (S) PF	47.50
1997 1 Peso, Peron (CN around B)	5.00
1994 50 Pesos, three coats of arms/book (G), PF	250.00
BAHAMAS	Unc.
1974 1 Cent, arms/starfish (B)	.50
1975 25 Cents, arms/sloop (N)	1.00
1974 50 Cents, arms/swordfish (CN)	2.00
1994 5 Dollars, arms/golf course (S), PF	4.50
1974 10 Dollars, arms/Milo Butler (CN)	12.00
2000 2 Dollars, Elizabeth II/Queen Mother (S), PF	50.00

Barbados 1996 5 Dollars

BARBADOS	Unc.
1973 1 Dollar, arms/flying fish (CN)	1.50
1970 4 Dollars, arms/plant (CN)	15.00
1996 5 Dollars, arms/royal couple (S), PF	40.00
1981 10 Dollars, arms/Neptune (CN)	12.50
1994 50 Dollars, arms/SIDS conference logo (G), PF	550.00

BELIZE	Unc.
1977 1 Cent, arms/swallow-tailed kite (AL, scalloped)	.75
1974 10 Cents, arms/hermit bird (CN)	2.00
1977 25 Cents, arms/motmot (CN)	3.00
1981 5 Dollars, arms/toucan (CN)	7.50
1982 100 Dollars, arms/kinkajou (G)	500.00
same but proof	200.00

BOLIVIA	VF
1909 5 Centavos, mountain scene/Caduceus (CN)	6.00
1935 10 Centavos, similar (CN)	1.00
1942 20 Centavos, similar (Z)	2.00

	Unc.
1951 5 Bolivianos, arms (C)	3.50
1951 10 Bolivianos, Bolivar/wreath (C)	4.50
1965 50 Centavos, mountain scene (N-clad St.)	1.75
1979 200 Pesos Bolivianos, arms/children (S), PF	16.50

BOLIVIA	Unc.
1991 10 Centavos, arms (St.)	.50
1987 20 Centavos, arms (St.)	.75
1991 50 Centavos, arms (St.)	.75
1998 1 Boliviano, arms/bank emblem (S), PF	70.00

REPUBLIC OF BRAZIL	VF
1918 50 Reis, female bust r. (CN)	.35
1918 100 Reis, similar (CN)	1.50
1938 200 Reis, Maua/locomotive (CN)	.75
1937 300 Reis, Gomes/harp (CN)	1.25
1937 400 Reis, Cruz/lamp (CN)	1.00
1936 1,000 Reis, Jose de Anchieta/open book (ALB)	1.00
1936 5,000 Reis, Dumont/wing (S)	4.00
1921 10,000 Reis, bust of Brazil/arms (G)	265.00
1947 20 Centavos, Vargas (ALB)	.15

	Unc.
1953 1 Cruzeiro, map of Brazil (ALB)	1.00
1957 1 Cruzeiro, arms (AL)	2.50

Republic of Brazil 1957 Cruzeiro

Republic of Brazil 1961 2 Cruzeiros

REPUBLIC OF BRAZIL	Unc.
1961 2 Cruzeiros, arms (AL)	1.00
1972 1 Cruzeiro, two portraits/map of Brazil (N)	1.65
1972 300 Cruzeiros, similar (G)	500.00
1980 5 Cruzeiros, coffee (St.)	.75
1988 100 Cruzados, child's portrait (St.)	3.00
1992 500 Cruzeiros, sea turtle (St.)	1.50
1993 5 Cruzeiros Reals, two parrots (St.)	1.50
1998 5 Centavos, bust of Tiradentes (C-plated St.)	.45
1999 1 Real, portrait (B around CN)	2.75
(1995) 3 Reais, BC30/Jerusalem Cross (S), PF	40.00
CHILE	**VF**
1904 1 Centavo, bust/wreath (C)	1.50
1915 5 Centavos, condor/wreath (S)	3.00
1938 10 Centavos, same (CN)	.50
1922 20 Centavos, similar (CN)	1.00
1933 1 Peso, similar (CN)	.75
(1903-05) 2 Pesos token, Compania de Salitres.../CSA monogram (vulcanite, various colors)	5.00
(1900-10) 2 Pesos token, Oficina Brac/$2 (vulcanite, green/brown)	6.50
1916 20 Centavos token, bust of girl (CN)	5.00
	Unc.
1946 100 Pesos, female bust l./arms (G)	575.00

CHILE	Unc.
1975 10 Centavos, condor (ALB)	.25
1975 1 Peso, O'Higgins (CN)	.25
1980 5 Pesos, Liberty breaking chains (CN)	2.00
1976 10 Pesos	1.25
1995 100 Pesos, arms (ALB)	2.50

COLOMBIA	VF
1918 1 Centavo, Liberty (CN)	15.00
1921 2 Centavos, similar (CN)	5.00
1933 2 Centavos	10.00
1935 5 Centavos, similar (CN)	1.75
1942 10 Centavos, Bolivar/arms (S)	1.50
Leprosarium 1921 2 Centavos, cross inscribed "LAZARETO" (CN)	6.75

The above coin was struck for use inside government-run leper colonies. Brazil, Costa Rica, Panama, and Venezuela also struck such pieces.

	Unc.
1971 20 Centavos, Santander (N-clad St.)	.35
1965 50 Centavos, Gaitan/arms (CN)	1.50
1956 1 Peso, old mint doors/arms (S)	25.00
1919 5 Pesos, stone cutter/arms (G)	215.00
1981 10 Pesos, equestrian statue/map (CNZ)	1.25
1993 500 Pesos, tree (CN around ALB)	4.00

COSTA RICA	VF
1903 2 Centimos (CN)	1.00
1936 5 Centimos, arms/wreath (B)	.75
1948 25 Centimos, similar (CN)	.20
1954 1 Colon, similar (St.)	.35
	Unc.
1982 25 Centimos, similar (AL)	.25
1970 5 Colones, arms/Renaissance portrait (S), PF	22.50
1997 5 Colones, arms/value (B)	.50
1970 20 Colones, Venus de Milo (S), PF	42.50
1974 50 Colones, arms/sea turtle (S)	22.50
1997 50 Colones, arms (B)	3.00
2000 500 Colones, arms/bank (B)	3.50

Cuba 1993 5 Pesos

CUBA	VF
1916 2 Centavos, arms/star (CN)	1.25
1943 5 Centavos, similar (B)	1.00
1915 10 Centavos, similar (S)	4.00
1920 20 Centavos, similar (S)	4.00
1916 40 Centavos, similar (S)	75.00
1952 40 Centavos, lighthouse and flag/tree growing through wheel (S)	6.00
1953 50 Centavos, Marti/scroll (S)	7.00
1932 1 Peso, arms/star (S)	16.50
1916 2 Pesos, Marti/arms (G)	85.00
1916 10 Pesos, similar (G)	450.00
	Unc.
1963 1 Centavo, arms/star (AL)	.60
1972 20 Centavos, similar (AL)	2.50
1982 1 Peso, Don Quixote and Sancho Panza/arms (CN)	9.00
1990 3 Pesos, Che Guevara/arms (CN)	6.00
1987 5 Pesos, slave breaking chains/arms (S)	32.50
1993 5 Pesos, ship/arms (S), PF	18.00
1993 20 Pesos, Castro/arms (S), PF	90.00

DOMINICAN REPUBLIC	VF
1937 1 Centavo, arms/palm tree (C)	1.50
1942 10 Centavos, arms/Indian head (S)	2.00
1956 25 Centavos, similar (S)	2.50
	Unc.
1955 1 Peso, arms/Trujillo (S)	25.00
1984 1 Centavo, arms/Caonabo (C-plated Z)	.25
1991 25 Centavos, arms/horse cart (N-clad St.)	.60
1967 1/2 Peso, similar (CN)	1.50
1976 1 Peso, arms/Duarte (CN)	2.00
1983 1 Peso, arms/three portraits (CN, polygonal)	2.50
1979 100 Pesos, arms/pope (G)	320.00
ECUADOR	VF
1909 1 Centavo, arms/wreath (CN)	9.00
1912 1/2 Decimo, Sucre/arms (S)	3.00
1928 10 Centavos, arms/bust (N)	2.00
1937 20 Centavos, arms/wreath (N)	.50
1928 50 Centavos, Sucre/arms (S)	3.00
	Unc.
1928 1 Condor, bust/arms (G)	350.00
1943 5 Sucres, Sucre/arms (S)	16.50

ECUADOR	Unc.
1946 5 Centavos, arms/wreath (CN)	1.00
1964 10 Centavos, similar (N-clad St.)	.75
1979 50 Centavos, similar (N clad St.)	.75
1964 1 Sucre, arms/Sucre (N-clad St.)	.50
1988 same but smaller	.40
1991 10 Sucres, arms/ancient sculpture (N-clad St.)	1.00
2000 25 Centavos, De Olmedo (St.)	1.00
EL SALVADOR	VF
1904 1 Peso, arms/Columbus (S)	15.00
1914 5 Centavos, arms/wreath (S)	7.00
1942 1 Centavo, Morazán (C)	.50
1951 10 Centavos, similar (CN)	3.50
1953 25 Centavos, priest l./wreath (S)	1.50
	Unc.
1976 1 Centavo, Morazán (B)	.20
1970 50 Centavos, similar (N)	.60
1988 1 Colon, Columbus (St.)	2.25
1992 2,500 Colones, four interlocking hands (G)	400.00

El Salvador 1904 Peso

GUATEMALA	VF
1915 12-1/2 Centavos (C)	1.25
1923 5 Pesos, Barrios (B)	4.00
1932 1 Centavo, arms (B)	1.00
1993 1 Centavo. Las Casas (B)	.25
1949 5 Centavos, arms/tree (S)	1.50
1958 10 Centavos, arms/monolith (S)	1.50
	Unc.
1963 25 Centavos, arms/female portrait (S)	5.50
1978 25 Centavos, similar (CN)	1.00
1992 1 Quetzal, arms/Merida (S), PF	50.00

HAÏTI	VF
1904 5 Centimes, Pedro Nord-Alexis/arms (CN)	5.00
1906 10 Centimes, similar (CN)	3.00
1949 10 Centimes, Estime/arms (CN)	2.00
	Unc.
1953 10 Centimes, Paul Magliore/arms (CNZ)	5.00
1970 20 Centimes, Francois Duvalier/arms (CN)	.85
1981 50 Centimes, Jean-Claude Duvalier/plant (CN)	1.75
1986 50 Centimes, Peralte/arms (CN)	1.00
1995 50 Centimes, similar (N-clad St.)	1.25
1995 1 Gourde, fortress/arms (ALB)	1.75
1970 40 Gourdes, Emperior Dessalines/arms (G), PF	240.00

HONDURAS	VF
1907 1 Centavo, pyramid (C)	4.00
1912 2 Centavos, pyramid (C)	15.00
1922 1 Peso, Liberty/arms (G)	250.00
1939 1 Centavo, arms (C)	.75
1949 2 Centavos, arms (C)	.50
1934 1 Lempira, arms/Indian (S)	7.50
	Unc.
1956 5 Centavos, arms (CN)	.60
1967 50 Centavos, arms/Indian (CN)	1.25
1978 50 Centavos, arms/Indian (CN)	1.00
1992 100 Lempiras, arms/sailing ship (S), PF	60.00
1992 500 Lempiras, arms/Morazan (G), PF	340.00

Jamaica 1995 25 Dollars

JAMAICA	Unc.
1969 1 Cent, arms/ackee fruit (C)	.25
1977 10 Cents, arms/butterfly on plant (CN)	.40
1982 25 Cents, arms/hummingbird (CN)	1.50
1976 50 Cents, Marcus Garvey/arms (CN, polygonal)	1.50
1972 10 Dollars, Bustamante and Manley/arms (S)	30.00
1979 10 Dollars, arms/child (S), PF	17.00
1995 25 Dollars, parrots/arms (S), PF	45.00
1995 50 Dollars, Bob Marley/arms (S), PF	40.00

MEXICO (REPUBLIC, DECIMAL)	VF
1903C 1 Centavo, eagle (C)	12.50
1903M 1 Centavo, same (C)	3.00

Estados Unidos	XF
1916 1 Centavo, eagle (C)	170.00
1961 1 Centavo, eagle/wheat (B)	.15
1906 2 Centavos, eagle/2 over C (C)	23.00
1915 2 Centavos, similar but smaller (C) (The small 1915 coppers were struck by Zapata, the famous revolutionary.)	17.50
1941 2 Centavos, as 1906 2c	1.25
1907 5 Centavos, eagle (N)	12.00

Estados Unidos	XF
1927 5 Centavos, eagle/5 over C (C)	30.00
1937 5 Centavos, eagle/value in Aztec border (CN)	1.00
1944 5 Centavos, eagle/Josefa l. (C)	.35
1950 5 Centavos, eagle/Josefa r. (CN)	1.50
1974 5 Centavos, eagle/Josefa (B)	.15
1928 10 Centavos, eagle/cap and rays (S)	2.75
1935 10 Centavos, eagle/10 over C (C)	30.00
1936 10 Centavos, eagle/value in Aztec border (CN)	2.50
1967 10 Centavos, eagle/Juarez (C)	.15
1976 10 Centavos, eagle/corn (CN)	.20
1935 20 Centavos, eagle/20 over C (C)	10.00
1943 20 Centavos, eagle/cap and rays (S)	2.50
1964 20 Centavos, eagle/pyramid (C)	.40
1979 20 Centavos, eagle/Madero (CN)	.15
1983 20 Centavos, eagle/Olmec sculpture (C)	.25
1951 25 Centavos, eagle/balance scale (billon)	.80
1964 25 Centavos, eagle/Madero (CN)	.15
1919 50 Centavos, eagle/cap and rays (S)	22.50
1943 50 Centavos, similar (S)	4.25

Estados Unidos	XF
1950 50 Centavos, eagle/realistic portrait of Cuauhtemoc (billon)	1.85
1956 50 Centavos, eagle/stylized portrait of Cuauhtemoc (C)	1.50

	Unc.
1979 50 Centavos, similar (CN)	.50
1983 50 Centavos, eagle/Palenque face (St.)	1.50
1910 1 Peso, eagle/horsewoman (S) (Many examples of the above have been cleaned and, if so, are worth less.)	50.00 XF
1945 1 Peso, eagle/cap and rays (S)	6.00
1947 1 Peso, eagle/Morelos r. (S)	4.50
1950 1 Peso, eagle/Morelos 3/4 bust l. (billon)	7.00
1957 1 Peso, eagle/Juarez (billon)	12.50
1962 1 Peso, eagle/Morelos r. (billon)	1.75
1978 1 Peso, eagle/Morelos l. (CN)	1.00
1985 1 Peso, eagle/Morelos 3/4 bust r. (St.)	.50
1921 2 Pesos, eagle/Independence winged (S)	55.00 XF
1945 2 Pesos, eagle (G)	55.00
1945 2-1/2 Pesos, eagle/Hidalgo (G)	65.00
1955 5 Pesos, similar (G) (Almost all 1945 2 and 2-1/2 Pesos and 1955 5 Pesos are restrikes.)	125.00

Estados Unidos	Unc.
1948 5 Pesos, eagle/stylized portrait of Cuauhtemoc (S)	12.50
1953 5 Pesos, eagle/Hidalgo (S)	9.50
1955 5 Pesos, same but smaller (S)	7.00
1957 5 Pesos, Juarez (S)	13.50
1959 5 Pesos, Carranza (S)	7.00
1971 5 Pesos, eagle/Guerrero (CN)	2.50
1980 5 Pesos, eagle/Quetzalcoatl (CN)	1.75
1988 5 Pesos, eagle (B)	.25
1959 (1959-72) 10 Pesos, eagle/Hidalgo (G, 0.24 oz.)	240.00
1956 10 Pesos, eagle/Hidalgo (S)	12.25
1957 10 Pesos, eagle/Juarez (S)	45.00
1960 10 Pesos, eagle/Hidalgo and Madero (S)	12.50
1975 10 Pesos, eagle/Hidalgo (CN, heptagonal)	7.50
1988 10 Pesos, eagle/Hidalgo (St.)	.25
1959 (1960-96) 20 Pesos, eagle/Aztec calendar (G, 0.48 oz.)	500.00
1980 20 Pesos, eagle/Mayan figure (CN)	2.25
1988 20 Pesos, eagle/G. Victoria (B)	.45
1968 25 Pesos, eagle/Aztec, Olympic rings (S)	7.50
1972 25 Pesos, eagle/Juarez (S)	7.50
1921 (1947-72) 50 Pesos, eagle/wingedIndependence (G, 1.2 oz.)	1,150.00

Estados Unidos	Unc.
1988 50 Pesos, eagle/Juarez (St.)	1.25
1977 100 Pesos, eagle/Morelos (S)	9.25
1984 100 Pesos, eagle/Carranza (ALB)	2.50
1985 200 Pesos, eagle/four revolutionaries (CN)	3.00
1985 250 Pesos, eagle/soccer ball (G)	200.00
1987 500 Pesos, eagle/Madero (CN)	2.25
1988 1,000 Pesos, eagle/Juana de Asbaje (ALB)	4.25
1986 2,000 Pesos, eagle/soccer (G)	1,950.00
1988 5,000 Pesos, eagle/monument (CN)	7.75

Mexico, New Pesos 1993 10 New Pesos

New Pesos	Unc.
1992 5 Centavos, eagle (St.)	.20
1993 10 Centavos, eagle (St.)	.25
1994 20 Centavos, eagle/wreath (ALB)	.35
1995 50 Centavos, eagle (ALB)	.75
1992 1 New Peso, eagle/N$1 (St. around ALB)	1.50
1993 1 New Peso, eagle/warrior with eagle helmet (S)	10.00
1996 1 Peso, eagle/$1 (St. around ALB)	1.25
1993 2 New Pesos, eagle/N$2 (St. around ALB)	2.35
1997 2 Pesos, eagle/$2 (St. around ALB)	2.35
1992 5 New Pesos, eagle/N$5 (St. around ALB)	4.00
1998 5 Pesos, eagle/$5 (St. around ALB)	4.00
1993 10 New Pesos, eagle/Aztec image, N$10 (ALB around S)	7.50
1998 10 Pesos, similar (B around CNZ)	5.00
2000 10 Pesos, similar but AÑO 2000 (B around CN)	5.00

New Pesos	Unc.
1994 20 New Pesos, eagle/Hidalgo, N$20 (ALB around S)	12.00
2000 20 Pesos, eagle/Xiutecuhtli (B around CN)	15.00
2000 20 Pesos, eagle/Octavio Paz (B around CN)	15.00
1995 50 New Pesos, eagle/Niños Heroes, N$50 (ALB around S)	25.00

Bullion Issues (Silver)	BU
1991 1/20 oz., eagle/winged Independence	5.50
1991 1/10 oz., similar	7.50
1991 1/4 oz., similar	9.00
1991 1/2 oz., similar	12.00
1949 1 oz., coining press/balance scale	27.50
1978-80 1 oz., similar	25.00
1982 1 oz., eagle/winged Independence	27.00
2000 1 oz., eagle surrounded by 10 eagles/winged Independence	28.00
1996 2 oz., similar	35.00
1996 5 oz., similar	120.00

Mexico 1985 1 Oz. Silver Bullion Issue

Gold	BU
1987 1/20 oz., eagle/winged Independence	275.00
1987 1/15 oz., similar	275.00
1991-93 1/10 oz., similar	BV + 20 percent
1981-93 1/4 oz., similar	BV + 11 percent
1981-93 1/2 oz., similar	BV + 8 percent
1981-93 1 oz., similar	BV + 3 percent
1943 1.2057 oz., similar	1,075.00

Platinum	BU
1989 1/4 oz., similar, PF	450.00

Revolutionary Issues Aguascalientes	VF
1915 5 Centavos, eagle/cap and rays (C)	30.00
1915 20 Centavos, similar (C)	35.00

Atlixtac	VF
1915 10 Centavos, eagle/wreath (C)	8.00

Chihuahua	VF
1915 5 Centavos, cap and rays/5 over C (C)	4.00

Durango	VF
1914 1 Centavo, date/wreath (C)	8.00

Jalisco	VF
1915 2 Centavos, cap and rays/2 over C (C)	20.00

Oaxaca	VF
1915 1 Centavo, inscription (C, rectangular)	400.00
1915 5 Centavos, Juarez (C)	4.50

Puebla	VF
1915 10 Centavos, eagle/X over C (C)	17.50

NICARAGUA	VF
1912 1/2 Centavo, arms in triangle/wreath (C)	2.50
1928 1 Centavo, arms in triangle/wreath (C)	6.00
1936 5 Centavos, similar (CN)	3.00
1936 10 Centavos, Francisco Hernandez de Cordoba/sun over five mountains (S)	3.00
1946 25 Centavos, similar (CN)	4.00
1912 1 Cordoba, similar (S)	75.00

	Unc.
1954 50 Centavos, similar (CN)	15.00
1972 1 Cordoba, similar (CN)	4.00
1967 50 Cordobas, triangular arms/Ruben Dario (G)	850.00
1975 50 Cordobas, similar/U.S. Liberty Bell (S)	21.50
1974 5 Centavos, similar/value (AL)	.50
1980 50 Centavos, Sandino (CN)	1.75
1987 5 Cordobas, Sandino's hat (ALB)	4.00
1994 10 Centavos, triangular arms/dove flying over Nicaragua (St.)	.75
1997 1 Cordoba, triangular arms (N-clad St.)	2.50

PANAMA	VF
1907 1/2 Centesimo, Balboa (CN)	2.50
1937 1 Centesimo, Uracca (C)	5.00
1904 2-1/2 Centesimos, Balboa/arms (S, popularly called the "Panama Pill")	15.00
1929 2-1/2 Centesimos, Balboa (CN)	3.50
1904 5 Centesimos, Balboa/arms (S)	6.00
1930 1/10 Balboa, arms/Balboa (S)	4.00
1947 1/4 Balboa, similar (S)	3.00
1904 50 Centesimos, Balboa/arms (S)	75.00

	Unc.
1953 1 Centesimo, Uracca (C)	4.00
1966 1/10 Balboa, arms/Balboa (CN-clad C)	3.00
1971 1/2 Balboa, similar (S-clad billon), PF	6.00
1983 1/2 Balboa, similar (CN-clad C)	3.00
1947 1 Balboa, allegory of Panama standing with arms/Balboa (S)	18.00
1970 5 Balboas, discus thrower/arms (S)	22.00
1982 20 Balboas, Balboa up to knees in water/arms (S), PF	180.00
1999 100 Balboas, President Moscoso/Panama Canal (G), PF	300.00
1983 500 Balboas, butterfly/arms (G, scalloped), PF	750.00

PARAGUAY	VF
1903 5 Centavos, lion (CN)	8.00
1925 50 Centavos, star (CN)	1.50
1938 2 Pesos, star (AL)	1.50
	Unc.
1947 5 Centimos, passion flower (ALB)	2.00
1953 50 Centimos, lion/wreath (ALB, scalloped)	1.00
1975 5 Guaranies, woman with jar (St.)	.50
1988 50 Guaranies, Estigarribia/dam (St.)	1.00
1974 150 Guaranies, Einstein/arms (S), PF	85.00
1968 300 Guaranies, Stroessner/lion (S)	10.00
1997 500 Guaranies, Caballero/bank building (B-plated St.)	2.50

Peru 1955 100 Soles

PERU	VF
1901 1 Centavo, sun/two cornucopias (C)	3.00
1919 2 Centavos, similar (C)	.75
1921 10 Centavos, head of Peru/fern branch (CN)	.75
1945 10 Centavos, similar (B)	.50
1935 1/2 Sol, arms/Peru seated (S)	3.25
1951 1 Sol, arms (B)	.50

	Unc.
1966 1 Sol, arms/llama (B)	1.00
1972 10 Soles, arms/Amaru (CN)	1.25
1955 100 Soles, arms/Peru (G)	1,275.00
1973 100 Soles, arms/flower (S)	12.50
1984 100 Soles, Admiral Grau (B)	1.00
1987 1 Inti, arms/Admiral Grau (CN)	1.00
1986 100 Intis, Caceres/arms (S)	17.50
1991 5 Centimos, arms (B)	.45
1996 1 Nuevo Sol, miner and oil derrick/arms (S)	45.00
1997 1 Nuevo Sol, arms/Barrenechen (S), PF	55.00
1994 5 Nuevos Soles, arms/bird (St. around B)	6.50
1926 1 Libra, arms/Indian (G)	225.00

SURINAME	Unc.
1962 1 Cent, arms (C)	1.00
1987 100 Cents, arms (CN)	1.75
1985 25 Gulden, dove/fist on star (S)	60.00

TRINIDAD & TOBAGO	Unc.
1966 1 Cent, arms (C)	.15
1971 10 Cents, arms (CN)	.35
1979 50 Cents, steel drums (CN)	1.50
1973 1 Dollar, Cerico bird (CN)	5.50
1977 5 Dollars, arms/ibis (CN)	20.00
1982 10 Dollars, arms/flag (CN)	20.00
1994 10 Dollars, arms/bird (S), PF	40.00
1984 200 Dollars, arms/bank building (G), PF	175.00

Trinidad & Tobago 1977 5 Dollars

URUGUAY	VF
1901 1 Centesimo, sun (CN)	5.00
1924 2 Centesimos, sun (CN)	2.00
1936 5 Centesimos, sun (CN)	2.00
1930 10 Centesimos, head of Uruguay/cougar (ALB)	4.00
1917 50 Centesimos, arms/Artigas (S)	12.00
1942 1 Peso, Artigas/cougar (S)	4.50
Early 1900s 10 Centesimos, token of Villegas Bros., vineyard, Carmelo (B)	10.00
	XF
1948 2 Centesimos, sun (C)	1.00
1953 5 Centesimos, Artigas (CN)	.50
1960 5 Centesimos, Artigas (N-B)	.25

Uruguay 1942 Peso

URUGUAY	Unc.
1977 1 Centesimo, sun with face (AL)	.25
1977 5 Centesimos, bull (AL)	.50
1976 10 Centesimos, horse (ALB)	.80
1965 1 Peso, Artigas/arms (ALB)	1.00
1961 10 Pesos, Rizzello/wreath (S)	8.00
1981 2 Nuevos Pesos, five ears of grain (CNZ)	1.00
1989 10 Nuevos Pesos, sun (St.)	.45
1989 100 Nuevos Pesos, Gaucho (St.)	.75
1981 5,000 Nuevos Pesos, dam/Uruguayan and Argentine arms (S), PF	15.00
1994 2 Pesos Urugayos, Artigas (B)	1.50
2000 10 Pesos, Artigas (St. around B)	3.50
2000 250 Pesos Urugayos, couple on horse (S), PF	47.50

Uruguay 1953 5 Centesimos

Uruguay 1981 5,000 Neuvos Pesos

Uruguay 2000 10 Pesos

Venezuela 1945 2 Bolivares

VENEZUELA	VF
1921 5 Centimos, arms (CN)	4.00
1938 12-1/2 Centimos, arms (CN)	.30
1944 12-1/2 Centimos, arms (B)	4.50
1929 1/4 Bolivar, Bolivar/arms (S)	.60
1935 1/2 Bolivar, similar (S)	1.25
1911 1 Bolivar, similar (S)	5.00
1954 1 Bolivar, similar (S)	2.50
1945 2 Bolivares, similar (S)	4.75
1902 5 Bolivares, similar (S)	16.00
1936 5 Bolivares, similar (S)	13.50
1912 20 Bolivares, similar (G)	170.00
	Unc.
1983 5 Centimos, arms (N-clad St.)	.10
1971 10 Centimos, arms (CN)	.25
1977 25 Centimos, Bolivar/arms (N)	.25
1960 50 Centimos, similar (S)	2.00
1977 1 Bolivar, similar (N)	.65
1960 2 Bolivares, similar (S)	5.00
1977 5 Bolivares, similar (N)	1.50
1973 10 Bolivares, Bolivar in rounded rectangle/arms in rounded rectangle (S), PF	400.00
2000 20 Bolivares, Bolivar/arms (N-clad St.)	.25

VENEZUELA	Unc.
1975 50 Bolivares, arms/armadillo (S)	27.50
1980 75 Bolivares, Sucre/donkey running (S)	12.50
1983 100 Bolivares, Bolivar standing/building (S), PF	20.00
1975 500 Bolivares, Bolivar in rounded rectangle/oil wells in rounded rectangle (G), PF	13,000.00
1990 500 Bolivares, Jose Paez/arms (S), PF	25.00
1998 500 Bolivares, Bolivar/arms (St.)	1.20
1999 500 Bolivares, similar	1.50
Leprosarium 1913 1/8 Bolivar, Maracaibo/Bs 1/8 (B) The above coin was struck for use in government-run leper colonies. Brazil, Colombia, Costa Rica, and Panama also struck such pieces.	12.00 VF

Venezuela 1999 500 Bolivares

INDEX

Treat Your Coins Well

The Warman's line of coin folders, from Krause Publications, is the perfect choice for showcasing your U.S. coins. Within this series are folders for the most popular U.S. denominations including State Quarters, Presidential Dollars, and Jefferson Nickels, among others.

At just $4.99 each ($7.99 for select deluxe editions), these coin folders are a gift for yourself, your favorite coin collector or history buff, and are an investment you'll enjoy for years to come.

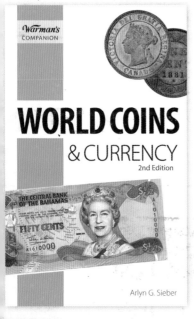